THE
REFERENCE
SHELF

ANIMAL RIGHTS and WELFARE

Edited by Jeanne Williams

THE REFERENCE SHELF

Volume 63, Number 4

THE H.W. WILSON COMPANY

New York   1991

THE REFERENCE SHELF

The books in this series contain reprints of articles, excerpts from books, and addresses on current issues and social trends in the United States and other countries. There are six separately bound numbers in each volume, all of which are generally published in the same calendar year. One number is a collection of recent speeches; each of the others is devoted to a single subject and gives background information and discussion from various points of view, concluding with a comprehensive bibliography that contains books and pamphlets and abstracts of additional articles on the subject. Books in the series may be purchased individually or on subscription.

Library of Congress Cataloging-in-Publication Data

Main entry under title:

Animal rights / edited by Jeanne Williams.
        p.   cm.—(The Reference shelf ; v. 63, no. 4)
    ISBN 0-8242-0815-3
    1. Animal rights.   2. Animal experimentation.   I. Williams,
Jeanne.   II. Series.
HV4708.A55   1991
179'.3—dc20   91-19053
                                                                                        CIP

Cover: Macaque monkeys who are being used for medical experiments at the New England Regional Primate Research Center in Southborough, Massachusetts. The facility is a part of Harvard Medical School.
Photo: AP/Wide World Photos

Printed in the United States of America

CONTENTS

PREFACE   7

I. RIGHTS AND RESPONSIBILITIES

EDITOR'S INTRODUCTION   9
Jean Bethke Elshtain. Why Worry About the Animals?
. . . .   The Progressive   10
Robert Wright. Are Animals People Too? . . . . .   The New
Republic   20
Gabriel Moran. Dominion Over the Earth
. . . .   Commonweal   31
Tim Stafford. Animal Lib . . . .   Christianity Today   40

II. ANIMALS IN RESEARCH

EDITOR'S INTRODUCTION   49
Geoffrey Cowley et al. Of Pain and Progress . .   Newsweek   50
Steve Siegel. Animal Research is Unnecessary and
Dangerous to Humans . . . .   Utne Reader   59
Frankie L. Trull. Animal Research is Critical to
Continued Progress in Human Health . . .   USA Today   63
Jerod M. Loeb et al. Human vs. Animal Rights . .   Journal
of the American Medical Association   70
Ron Karpati. A Scientist: "I Am the Enemy" . .   Newsweek   83
Alan M. Goldberg and John M. Frazier. Alternatives to
Animals in Toxicity Testing . . . . . .   Scientific American   85
Jane Goodall. A Plea for the Chimps . . . .   The New York
Times Magazine   95

III. THE MOVEMENT IN TRANSITION

EDITOR'S INTRODUCTION   103

Jeanie Kasindorf. The Fur Flies . . . .   New York   104
Richard Conniff. Superchicken . . . .   Discover   115
Michael Satchell. The American Hunter Under Fire
. . . .   U.S. News & World Report   124
Macdonald Daly. All Heaven in a Rage . . .   History Today   131
Richard Conniff. Fuzzy-Wuzzy Thinking About Animal
Rights . . . .   Audubon   135
Merritt Clifton. Out of the Cage . .   The Animals' Agenda   147

BIBLIOGRAPHY
Books and Pamphlets   157
Additional Periodical Articles with Abstracts   158

PREFACE

Over the millennia, humans have used animals for a variety of purposes: food, clothing, labor, transportation, war, hunting, magic, medicine, and companionship. For the most part, they could not have survived without doing so. The question of what constitutes proper treatment of animals has therefore been much debated by ethicists and moralists. What is our proper role with regard to nonhuman creatures? May we do as we like to them? Are we constrained from using them in some circumstances, but not in others? Or should our goal be complete separation between us and them, if such a thing were even possible?

The moral philosophers of both East and West have given these questions considerable attention. The book of Genesis in the Bible describes the paradise of Eden as a place where nature was perfectly benign, with no need for violence or predation even among animals. The Indian religions of Jainism and Buddhism stress the principle of *ahimsa,* or nonviolence toward all living things. But the Bible goes on to say that in the time of Noah humans succumbed to their urges and began eating animal flesh, and few people even in India are willing to adopt the extreme asceticism of Jain monks and nuns. Most religious systems and secular philosophies do not challenge the use of animals per se, but seek in various ways to arouse a sense of respect for their needs and to curb mistreatment of them.

These ancient questions are far from being resolved in our own day, when our relationship to the beasts has grown much more complex. To think about these questions is to contemplate humanity's unique and anomalous position: we live and die as animals do, we are molded by instinct and heredity just as they are, but we are also the products of civilization, emancipated from nature, living in a world mostly of our own making and with great power to create and destroy. Each year, billions of animals worldwide are killed in medical experiments, slaughtered for food, shot for sport, put to death in animal shelters, and endangered by manmade pollution and loss of habitat. Since we live in an era of liberation movements, when one group after another has tried to claim the moral attention of the world, it is not surprising to find a mass movement that makes similar claims on behalf of animals,

7

utilizing the same ethical arguments that previous groups have used. Still, the idea that legal rights can be extended to animals continues to strike many people as excessive, and the movement, despite its vigorous growth over the past two decades, has found it difficult to sway public opinion, except on a handful of popular issues such as the wearing of fur.

The campaign to achieve recognition of an inherent right of animals to live without human interference (or some modified form of that right) is the subject of the first section in this book. The second section examines in detail the confrontation between animal-rights activists and medical researchers over the use of sentient creatures in scientific experiments. The third section covers a variety of institutions that have come under attack by animal advocates, including factory farming, the fur industry, and blood sports; it also looks at the history of the movement and its prospects for the future.

The editor wishes to thank the authors and publishers who kindly granted permission to reprint the material in this collection. Acknowledgement of their permission is specified in footnotes at the beginning of every selection in this book.

JEANNE WILLIAMS

May 1991

I. RIGHTS AND RESPONSIBILITIES

EDITOR'S INTRODUCTION

When Thomas Jefferson asserted in the Declaration of Independence that it was a self-evident truth that men "are endowed by their Creator with certain unalienable Rights," he was stating what was even then a radical idea: that the fundamental rights, especially the right to live free from molestation and coercion, arise simply from the condition of being a man rather than by a political arrangement, such as a ruler's decree or a majority vote. It is far from being accepted worldwide even today, but in the United States this idea is the foundation of our identity as a nation and the means by which moral concerns are given political force. Successive categories of people who were once held to be "inferior" have appealed for reconsideration of their status on the basis of this tenet.

Within the last fifteen years, campaigns have been under way to make that tenet even more inclusive and to construe the idea of natural rights as applying to two additional categories of living beings, neither of which can make the claim on its own behalf: babies in the womb and animals. These attempts have been ridiculed, in both cases, as absurd. Yet, as the ethicist Peter Singer points out in his book *Animal Liberation,* the idea of women's rights was dismissed as equally absurd when Mary Wollstonecraft published *A Vindication of the Rights of Women* in 1792. In fact, one of her critics, the philosopher Thomas Taylor, drew a direct analogy between women and animals, declaring that if women have rights, so do animals, and for the same reasons.

The idea that animals, *by right,* should be free from molestation by humans gained a measure of acceptance only after the publication of Singer's book in 1975. Since that time, the membership of groups dedicated to achieving recognition of these rights has grown to such a degree that people with a vested interest in the use of animals—including medical researchers, farmers, hunters, and trappers—now perceive the movement as a real threat. In the first article reprinted here, "Why Worry About the Animals?," Jean Bethke Elshtain traces the recent develop-

9

ment of the movement and identifies the reasons for its emergence in the 1980s.

The philosophical foundations of the animal-rights movement are discussed and evaluated from two perspectives in the second and third selections, "Are Animals People Too?" by Robert Wright and "Dominion Over the Earth" by Gabriel Moran. Both authors reject Singer's idea of the absolute equality of all animals, an idea subscribed to only by the most radical wing of the movement. But both conclude—one for humanist and the other for religious reasons—that the suffering of animals who are forced to serve human needs is a matter of serious moral concern, requiring fine moral distinctions. Tim Stafford, in "Animal Lib," discusses the issue in light of the biblical idea that human beings bear responsibility for thoughtful stewardship of the earth and its creatures.

The possibility raised by some ethicists of extending the protection of the Constitution to animals is one of the subjects of the fifth selection, a forum discussion that sets forth some of the movement's most powerful arguments as well as some of its hopeless inconsistencies. The participants include a prominent animal-rights advocate, a lawyer active in animal-rights cases, a constitutional law scholar, and a specialist in biomedical ethics.

WHY WORRY ABOUT THE ANIMALS?[1]

These things are happening or have happened recently:

• The wings of seventy-four mallard ducks are snapped to see whether crippled birds can survive in the wild. (They can't.)

• Infant monkeys are deafened to study their social behavior, or turned into amphetamine addicts to see what happens to their stress level.

• Monkeys are separated from their mothers, kept in isolation, addicted to drugs, and induced to commit "aggressive" acts.

[1]Reprint of an article by Jean Bethke Elshtain, Centennial Professor of Political Science at Vanderbilt University. *The Progressive*. 54:17-8+. Mr '90. Copyright 1990 by The Progressive, Inc.

• Pigs are blowtorched and observed to see how they respond to third-degree burns. No pain-killers are used.

• Monkeys are immersed in water and vibrated to cause brain damage.

• For thirteen years, baboons have their brains bashed at the University of Pennsylvania as research assistants laugh at signs of the animals' distress.

• Monkeys are dipped in boiling water; other animals are shot in the face with high-powered rifles.

The list of cruelties committed in the name of "science" or "research" could be expanded endlessly. "Fully 80 per cent of the experiments involving rhesus monkeys are either unnecessary, represent useless duplication of previous work, or could utilize nonanimal alternatives," says John F. McArdle, a biologist and specialist in primates at Illinois Wesleyan University.

Growing awareness of animal abuse is helping to build an increasingly militant animal-welfare movement in this country and abroad—a movement that is beginning to have an impact on public policy. Secretary of Health and Human Services Frederick Goodwin complained recently that complying with new Federal regulations on the use—or abuse—of animals will drain off some 17 per cent of the research funds appropriated to the National Institutes of Health. (It is cheaper to purchase, use, and destroy animals than to retool for alternative procedures.) One of the institutes, the National Institute of Mental Health, spends about $30 million a year on research that involves pain and suffering for animals.

The new animal-welfare activists are drawing attention in part because of the tactics they espouse. Many preach and practice civil disobedience, violating laws against, say, breaking and entering. Some have been known to resort to violence against property and—on a few occasions—against humans.

Some individuals and groups have always fretted about human responsibility toward nonhuman creatures. In the ancient world, the historian Plutarch and the philosopher Porphyry were among those who insisted that human excellence embodied a refusal to inflict unnecessary suffering on all other creatures, human and nonhuman.

But with the emergence of the Western rationalist tradition, animals lost the philosophic struggle. Two of that tradition's great exponents, René Descartes and Immanuel Kant, dismissed out of hand the moral worth of animals. Descartes's view, which has brought comfort to every human who decides to confine, poison, cripple, infect, or dismember animals in the interest of human knowledge, was the more extreme: He held that animals are simply machines, devoid of consciousness or feeling. Kant, more sophisticated in his ethical reasoning, knew that animals could suffer but denied that they were self-conscious. Therefore, he argued, they could aptly serve as means to human ends.

To make sure that human sensibilities would not be troubled by the groans, cries, and yelps of suffering animals—which might lead some to suspect that animals not only bleed but feel pain—researchers have for a century subjected dogs and other animals to an operation called a centriculocordectomy, which destroys their vocal chords.

Still, there have long been groups that placed the suffering of animals within the bounds of human concern. In the nineteenth and early twentieth centuries, such reform movements as women's suffrage and abolitionism made common cause with societies for the prevention of cruelty to animals. On one occasion in 1907, British suffragettes, trade-unionists, and their animal-welfare allies battled London University medical students in a riot triggered by the vivisection of a dog.

Traditionally, such concern has been charitable and, frequently, highly sentimental. Those who perpetrated the worst abuses against animals were denounced for their "beastly" behavior—the farmer who beat or starved his horse; the householder who chained and kicked his dog; the aristocratic hunter who, with his guests, slew birds by the thousands in a single day on his private game preserve.

For the most part, however, animals have been viewed, even by those with "humane" concerns, as means to human ends. The charitable impulse, therefore, had a rather condescending, patronizing air: Alas, the poor creatures deserve our pity.

The new animal-welfare movement incorporates those historic concerns but steers them in new directions. Philosophically, animal-rights activists seek to close the gap between "human" and "beast," challenging the entire Western rationalist tradition which holds that the ability to reason abstractly is *the* defining human attribute. (In that tradition, women were often located on a scale somewhere between "man" and "beast," being deemed human but not quite rational.)

Politically, the new abolitionists, as many animal-welfare activists call themselves, eschew sentimentalism in favor of a tough-minded, insistent claim that animals, too, have rights, and that violating those rights constitutes oppression. It follows that animals must be liberated—and since they cannot liberate themselves in the face of overwhelming human hegemony, they require the help of liberators much as slaves did in the last century.

Thus, the rise of vocal movements for animal well-being has strong historic antecedents. What is remarkable about the current proliferation of efforts is their scope and diversity. Some proclaim animal "rights." Others speak of animal "welfare" or "protection." Still others find the term "equality" most apt, arguing that we should have "equal concern" for the needs of all sentient creatures.

When so many issues clamor for our attention, when so many problems demand our best attempts at fair-minded solution, why animals, why now? There is no simple explanation for the explosion of concern, but it is clearly linked to themes of peace and justice. Perhaps it can be summed up this way: Those who are troubled by the question of who is or is not within the circle of moral concern; those who are made queasy by our use and abuse of living beings for our own ends; those whose dreams of a better world are animated by some notion of a peaceable kingdom, *should* consider our relationship with the creatures that inhabit our planet with us—the creatures that have helped sustain us and that may share a similar fate with us unless we find ways to deflect if not altogether end the destruction of our earthly habitat.

Dozens of organizations have sprung up, operating alongside—and sometimes in conflict with—such older mainline outfits as the Humane Society, the Anti-Vivisection League, and the World Wildlife Fund. Among the new groups are People for the Ethical Treatment of Animals (PETA), Trans-Species Unlimited, In Defense of Animals, the Gorilla Foundation, Primarily Primates, Humane Farming Association, Farm Animal Reform, Alliance for Animals, Citizens to End Animal Suffering and Exploitation (CEASE), Whale Adoption Project, Digit Fund—the list goes on and on.

Some organizations focus on the plight of animals on factory farms, especially the condition of anemic, imprisoned veal calves kept in darkness and unable to turn around until they are killed at fourteen weeks. Others are primarily concerned with conditions in the wild, where the habitat of the panda, among others, is being destroyed or where great and wonderful creatures like the black rhinoceros and the African elephant or magnificent cats like the snow leopard or the Siberian tiger are marching toward extinction, victims of greedy buyers of illegal tusks or pelts.

Another group of activists clusters around the use of animals in such profitable pursuits as greyhound racing, where dogs by the hundreds are destroyed once they cease "earning their keep," or in tourist attractions where such wonderfully intelligent social beings as the orca and the dolphin are tuned into circus freaks for profit. In the wild, orcas can live for up to 100 years; in captivity, the average, sadly misnamed "killer whale" lasts about five.

Those wonderful chimpanzees that have been taught to speak to us through sign-language also arouse concern. If the funding ends or a researcher loses interest, they are sometimes killed, sometimes turned over to the less-than-tender mercies of laboratory researchers to be addicted to cocaine, infected with a virus, or subjected to some other terrible fate. Eugene Linden describes, in his study *Silent Partners*, chimps desperately trying to convey their pain and fear and sadness to uncomprehending experimenters.

Use of animals in war research is an industry in itself, though one usually shielded from public view. Monkeys are the most likely subjects of experiments designed to measure the effects of neutron-bomb radiation and the toxicity of chemical-warfare agents. Beginning in 1957, monkeys were placed at varying distances from ground zero during atomic testing; those that didn't die immediately were encaged so that the "progress" of their various cancers might be noted.

Radiation experiments on primates continue. Monkeys' eyes are irradiated, and the animals are subjected to shocks of up to 1,200 volts. Junior researchers are assigned the "death watch," and what they see are primates so distressed that they claw at themselves and even bit hunks from their own arms or legs in a futile attempt to stem the pain. At a Government proving ground in Aberdeen, Maryland, monkeys are exposed to chemical-warfare agents.

Dolphins, animals of exquisite intelligence, have been trained by the military in such scenarios as injecting carbon dioxide cartridges into Vietnamese divers and planting and removing mines.

The Navy announced in April 1989 that it would continue its $30 million clandestine program, expanded in the Reagan years, to put dolphins to military use. The aim, *The New York Times* reported, is to use dolphins captured in the Gulf of Mexico to guard the Trident Nuclear Submarine Base at Bangor, Washington.

Several years ago, when I was writing a book on women and war, I came across references to the use of dogs in Vietnam. When I called the Pentagon and was put through to the chief of military history, Southeast Asia Branch, he told me that no books existed on the subject, but he did send me an excerpt from the *Vietnam War Almanac* that stated the U.S. military "made extensive use of dogs for a variety of duties in Vietnam, including scouting, mine detecting, tracking, sentry duty, flushing out tunnels, and drug detecting." Evidently, many of these dogs were killed rather than returned home, since it was feared their military training ill-suited them for civilian life.

Much better known, because of an increasingly successful animal-rights campaign, is the use of animals to test such household products as furniture polish and such cosmetics as shampoo and lipstick.

For years, industry has determined the toxicity of floor wax and detergents by injecting various substances into the stomachs of beagles, rabbits, and calves, producing vomiting, convulsions, respiratory illness, and paralysis. The so-called LD (lethal dose) 50 test ends only when half the animals in a test group have died. No anesthesia or pain killers are administered.

Dr. Andrew Rowan, assistant dean of the Tufts University School of Medicine, has offered persuasive evidence that such testing methods are crude and innaccurate measures of a product's safety. For one thing, a number of potentially significant variables, including the stress of laboratory living, are not taken into account, thus tainting any comparison of the effect of a given substance on human consumers.

The LD50 is notoriously unreproducible; the method for rating irritation is extremely subjective; and interspecies variations make test results highly suspect when applied to the human organism.

Most notorious of the "tests" deployed by the multibillion-dollar cosmetics industry is the Draize, which has been used since the 1940s to measure the potential irritative effects of products. Rabbits—used because their eyes do not produce tears and, therefore, cannot cleanse themselves—are placed into stocks and their eyes are filled with foreign substances. When a rabbit's eyes ulcerate—again, no pain killers are used—the cosmetic testers (who are usually not trained laboratory researchers) report a result. To call this procedure "scientific" is to demean authentic science.

Curiously, neither the LD50 test nor the Draize are required by law. They continue in use because manufacturers want to avoid alarming consumers by placing warning labels on products. More accurate methods available include computer simulations to measure toxicity, cell-culture systems, and organ-culture tests that use chicken-egg membranes.

The disdainful response by corporate America to animal-protection concerns seems, at least in this area, to be undergoing a slow shift toward new laboratory techniques that abandon wasteful, crude, and cruel animal testing. Several large cosmetics manufacturers, including Revlon, have only recently announced that they will phase out animal testing, confirming the claim of animal-welfare groups that the tests are unnecessary.

Among the nastier issues in the forefront of the "animal wars" is the controversy over hunting and trapping.

It's estimated that about seventeen million fur-bearing animals (plus "trash" animals—including pets—the trapper doesn't want) are mangled each year in steel-jaw leg-hold traps that tear an animal's flesh and break its bones. Many die of shock or starvation before the trapper returns. Some animals chew off part of a limb in order to escape. More than sixty countries now ban the leg-hold trap, requiring the use of less painful and damaging devices.

Protests against the manufacture, sale, and wearing of fur coats have been aggressively—and successfully—mounted in Western Europe. In Holland, fur sales have dropped 80 per cent in the last few years. Radical groups in Sweden have broken into fur farms to release minks and foxes. An effort to shame women who wear fur has had enormous impact in Great Britain.

Similar campaigns have been mounted in the United States, but the fur industry is waging a well-financed counterattack in this country. Curiously, the industry's efforts have been tacitly supported by some rights-absolutists within feminism who see wearing a fur coat as a woman's right. It's difficult to think of a greater *reductio ad absurdum* of the notion of "freedom of choice," but it seems to appeal to certain adherents of upwardly mobile, choice-obsessed political orthodoxy.

Hunting may be the final frontier for animal-welfare groups. Because hunting is tied to the right to bear arms, any criticism of hunting is construed as an attack on constitutional freedoms by hunting and gun organizations, including the powerful and effective National Rifle Association. A bumper sticker I saw on a pick-up truck in Northampton, Massachusetts, may tell the tale: MY WIFE, YES. MY DOG, MAYBE. BUT MY GUN, NEVER.

For some animal protectionists, the case against hunting is open and shut. They argue that the vast majority of the estimated 170 million animals shot to death in any given year are killed for blood sport, not for food, and that the offspring of these slaughtered creatures are left to die of exposure or starvation. Defenders of blood sports see them as a skill and a tradition, a lingering relic of America's great frontier past. Others—from nineteenth century feminists to the Norman Mailer of *Why Are We in Vietnam?*—link the national mania for hunting with a deeper thirst for violence.

I am not convinced there is an inherent connection between animal killing and a more general lust for violence, but some disquieting evidence is beginning to accumulate. Battered and abused women in rural areas often testify, for example, that their spouses also abused animals, especially cows, by stabbing them with pitchforks, twisting their ears, kicking them, or, in one reported incident, using a board with a nail in it to beat a cow to death.

But even people who recoil from hunting and other abuses of animals often find it difficult to condemn such experiments as those cited at the beginning of this article, which are, after all, conducted to serve "science" and, perhaps, to alleviate human pain and suffering. Sorting out this issue is no easy task if one is neither an absolute prohibitionist nor a relentless defender of the scientific establishment. When gross abuses come to light, they are often reported in ways that allow and encourage us to distance ourselves from emotional and ethical involvement. Thus the case of the baboons whose brains were bashed in at the University of Pennsylvania prompted *The New York Times* to editorialize, on July 31, 1985, that the animals "seemed" to be suffering. They *were* suffering, and thousands of animals suffer every day.

Reasonable people should be able to agree on this: that alternatives to research that involves animal suffering must be vigorously sought; that there is no excuse for such conditions as dogs lying with open incisions, their entrails exposed, or monkeys with untreated, protruding broken bones, exposed muscle tissue, and infected wounds, living in grossly unsanitary conditions amidst feces and rotting food; that quick euthanasia should be administered to a suffering animal after the conclusion of a pain-inducing procedure; that pre- and post-surgical care must be provided for animals; that research should not be needlessly duplicated, thereby wasting animal lives, desensitizing generations of researchers, and flushing tax dollars down the drain.

What stands in the way of change? Old habits, bad science, unreflective cruelty, profit, and, in some cases, a genuine fear that animal-welfare groups want to stop all research dead in its tracks. "Scientists fear shackles on research," intones one report. But why are scientists so reluctant to promote such research alternatives as modeling, in-vitro techniques, and the use of lower organisms? Because they fear that the public may gain wider knowledge of what goes on behind the laboratory door. Surely those using animals should be able to explain themselves and to justify their expenditure of the lives, bodies, and minds of other creatures.

There is, to be sure, no justification for the harassment and terror tactics used by some animal-welfare groups. But the scientist who is offended when an animal-welfare proponent asks, "How would you feel if someone treated your child the way you treat laboratory animals?" should ponder one of the great ironies in the continuing debate: Research on animals is justified on grounds that they are "so like us."

I *do* appreciate the ethical dilemma here. As a former victim of polio, I have thought long and hard for years about animal research and human welfare. This is where I come down, at least for now:

First, most human suffering in this world cannot be ameliorated in any way by animal experimentation. Laboratory infliction of suffering on animals will not keep people healthy in Asia, Africa, and Latin America. As philosopher Peter Singer has argued, we already know how to cure what ails people in desperate poverty; they need "adequate nutrition, sanitation, and health care. It has been estimated that 250,000 children die each week around the world, and that one quarter of these deaths are by dehydration due to diarrhea. A simple treatment, already known and needing no animal experimentation, could prevent the deaths of these children."

Second, it is not clear that a cure for terrible and thus far incurable diseases such as AIDS is best promoted with animal experimentation. Some American experts on AIDS admit that French scientists are making more rapid progress toward a vaccine because they are working directly with human volunteers, a course of action Larry Kramer, a gay activist, has urged upon American scientists. Americans have been trying since 1984 to infect chimpanzees with AIDS, but after the expenditure of millions of dollars, AIDS has not been induced in any nonhuman animal. Why continue down this obviously flawed route?

Third, we could surely agree that a new lipstick color, or an even more dazzling floor wax, should never be promoted for profit over the wounded bodies of animals. The vast majority of creatures tortured and killed each year suffer for *nonmedical* reasons. Once this abuse is eliminated, the really hard cases having to do with human medical advance and welfare can be debated, item by item.

Finally, what is at stake is the exhaustion of the eighteenth century model of humanity's relationship to nature, which had, in the words of philosopher Mary Midgley, "built into it a bold, contemptuous rejection of the nonhuman world."

Confronted as we are with genetic engineering and a new eugenics, with the transformation of farms where animals ranged freely into giant factories where animals are processed and produced like objects, with callous behavior on a scale never before imagined under the rubric of "science," we can and must do better than to dismiss those who care as irrational and emotional animal-lovers who are thinking with their hearts (not surprisingly, their ranks are heavily filled with women), and who are out to put a stop to the forward march of rationalism and science.

We humans do not deserve peace of mind on this issue. Our sleep should be troubled and our days riddled with ethical difficulties as we come to realize the terrible toll one definition of "progress" has taken on our fellow creatures.

We must consider our meat-eating habits as well. Meat-eating is one of the most volatile, because most personal, of all animal-welfare questions. Meat-eaters do not consider themselves immoral, though hard-core vegetarians find meat-eating repugnant—the consumption of corpses. Such feminist theorists as Carol Adams insist that there is a connection between the butchering of animals and the historic maltreatment of women. Certainly, there is a politics of meat that belongs on the agenda along with other animal-welfare issues.

I, for one, do not believe humans and animals have identical rights. But I do believe that creatures who can reason in their own ways, who can suffer, who are mortal beings like ourselves, have a value and dignity we must take into account. Animals are not simply a means to our ends.

When I was sixteen years old, I journeyed on a yellow school bus from LaPorte, Colorado, to Fairbanks, Iowa, on a 4-H Club "exchange trip." On the itinerary was a visit to a meat-packing plant in Des Moines. As vivid as the day I witnessed it is the scene I replay of men in blood-drenched coats "bleeding" pigs strung up by their heels on a slowly moving conveyer belt. The pigs—bright and sensitive creatures, as any person who has ever met one knows—were screaming in terror before the sharp, thin blade entered their jugular veins. They continued to struggle and squeal until they writhed and fell silent.

The men in the slaughter room wore boots. The floor was awash in blood. I was horrified. But I told myself this was something I should remember. For a few months I refused to eat pork. But then I fell back into old habits—this was Colorado farm country in the late 1950s, after all.

But at one point, a few years ago, that scene and those cries of terror returned. This time I decided I would not forget, even though I knew my peace of mind would forever be disturbed.

ARE ANIMALS PEOPLE TOO?[2]

I recently interviewed several animal rights activists in hopes that they would say some amusing, crazy-sounding things that might liven up this article. More often than not I was disappointed. They would come close to making unreservedly extremist pronouncements but then step back from the brink, leaving me with a quote that was merely provocative. For example, Ingrid

[2]Reprint of an article by Robert Wright. *The New Republic.* 202:20+. Mr 12 '90. Copyright 1990 by The New Republic, Inc.

Newkirk, co-founder of People for the Ethical Treatment of Animals (PETA), seemed on the verge of conceding that Frank Perdue is no better than Adolf Hitler—a proposition that technically follows from her premise that animals possess the moral status of humans (and from references in animal rights literature to the ongoing "animal holocaust"). But she wouldn't go all the way. "He's the animals' Hitler, I'll give you that," she said. "If you were a chicken . . . you wouldn't think he was Mother Teresa." The other cofounder of PETA, Alex Pacheco, was not much more helpful. "You and I are equal to the lobsters when it comes to being boiled alive," he said, raising my hopes. But, he added, "I don't mean I couldn't decide which one to throw in, myself or the lobster."

The biggest disappointment was a woman who went by the pseudonym "Helen." She was a member of the Animal Liberation Front, a shadowy group that goes around breaking into scientific laboratories, documenting the conditions therein, and sometimes burning down the labs (minus the animals, which are typically "liberated"—taken somewhere else—in the process). Given all the intrigue involved in interviewing "Helen"—I had to "put out the word" that I wanted to talk with an ALF member, and when she called she always used a streetside phone booth and never left a number—I expected a rich encounter. This hope grew when I found out that she had participated in a recent lab-burning at the University of Arizona. But as professed arsonists go, Helen seemed like a very nice and fairly reasonable person. She was a combination of earnest moral anguish ("For the most part, people just aren't aware of how much suffering and death goes into what they eat and wear. . . . Most people just literally don't know") and crisp professionalism ("Whether I have any animosity toward [laboratory researchers] is irrelevant. . . . I just do everything I can to move them into a different job category"). And though her reverence for life may strike you as creepy—she picks up spiders off the floor and moves them outdoors, rather than squash them—it is not unbounded. She assured me that if termites were destroying her home, she would call an exterminator.

One reason for this general failure to gather satisfactorily extremist quotes is that animal rights activists have become more media-savvy, developing a surer sense for when they are being baited. But another reason is my own failure to find their ideas extremist. Slowly I seem to be getting drawn into the logic of animal rights. I still eat meat, wear a leather belt, and support the use of animals in important scientific research. But not without a certain amount of cognitive dissonance.

The animal rights movement, which has mushroomed during the past decade, most conspicuously in the growth of PETA (membership around 300,000), is distinguished from the animal welfare movement, as represented by, for example, the Humane Society of the United States. Animal *welfare* activists don't necessarily claim that animals are the moral equivalent of humans, just that animals' feelings deserve some consideration; we shouldn't needlessly hurt them—with pointless experimentation, say, or by making fur coats. And just about every thinking person, if pressed, will agree that animal welfare is a legitimate idea. Hardly anyone believes in kicking dogs.

But the truth is that animal welfare is just the top of a slippery slope that leads to animals rights. Once you buy the premise that animals can experience pain and pleasure, and that their welfare therefore deserves *some* consideration, you're on the road to comparing yourself with a lobster. There may be some exit ramps along the way—plausible places to separate welfare from rights—but I can't find any. And if you don't manage to find one, you wind up not only with a rather more sanguine view of animal rights but also with a more cynical view of the concept of human rights and its historical evolution.

None of this is to say that a few minutes of philosophical reflection will lead you to start wearing dumpling-shaped fake-leather shoes, sporting a "Meat is Murder" button, or referring to your pet dog as your "companion animal." The stereotype about the people who do these things—that they're ill at ease in human society, even downright antagonistic toward other humans—is generally wrong, but the stereotype that they're, well, *different* from most people is not. These are dyed-in-the-wool activists, and if they weren't throwing themselves into this cause, they would probably be throwing themselves into some other cause. (Pacheco, for example, had originally planned to become a priest.) Moreover, very few of them were converted to the movement solely or mainly via philosophy. Many will say they were critically influenced by the book *Animal Liberation* (1975), written by the Australian ethicist Peter Singer, but reading Singer was for most of them merely a ratifying experience, a seal of philosophical approval for their intuitive revulsion at animal suffering. Pacheco

received a copy of the book the same week he got grossed out
while touring a Canadian slaughterhouse. He later gave a copy to
Newkirk, who was then chief of Animal Disease Control for the
District of Columbia. Around that time she spent a day trying to
rescue some starving, neglected horses that were locked in their
stalls and mired in mud. That's when it hit her: "It didn't make
sense. I had spent the whole day trying to get some starving
horses out of a stall and here I was going home to eat some other
animal." This gut perception is a recurring theme, as crystallized
by Helen: "I just realized that if I wouldn't eat my dog, why
should I eat a cow?"

Good question. And implicit in it is the core of the case for
animal rights: the modest claim—not disputed by anyone who
has ever owned a dog or cat, so far as I know—that animals are
sentient beings, capable of pleasure and pain. People who would
confine natural rights to humans commonly talk about the things
we have that animals don't—complex language, sophisticated
reasoning, a highly evolved culture. But none of these is important, for moral purposes, in the way that sheer sentience is.

One way to appreciate this is through a simple thought experiment. Suppose there's a planet populated by organisms that look
and act exactly like humans. They walk, talk, flirt, go to law
school, blush in response to embarrassing comments, and discuss
their impending deaths in glum tones. Now suppose it turns out
they're automatons, made out of silicon chips—or even made out
of flesh and blood. The important thing is that all their behavior—their blushing, their discussion of death—is entirely a product of the physical circuitry inside their heads and isn't accom-
panied by any subjective experience; they can't feel pain,
pleasure, or anything else. In other words (to use the terminology
of Thomas Nagel), it isn't like anything to be them.

Is there anything particularly immoral about slapping one of
them in the face? Most everyone would say: obviously not, since it
doesn't hurt. How about killing one of them? Again, no; their
death doesn't preclude their future experience of happiness, as
with real live humans, or cause any pain for friends and relatives.
There is no apparent reason to bestow any moral status whatsoever on these creatures, much less the exalted status that the
human species now enjoys. They have powerful brains, complex
language, and high culture, but none of this makes them
significant.

Now rearrange the variables: subtract all these attributes and add sentience. In other words, take all the robots off the planet and populate it with non-human animals: chimps, armadillos, dogs, etc. Is there anything immoral about gratuitously hurting or killing one of these? Do they have individual rights? Most people would answer yes to the first question, and some would answer yes to the second. But the main point is that few people would quickly and easily say "no" to either, because these are harder questions than the robot question. Sentience lies at the core of our moral thinking, and language, intelligence, etc., lie nearer the periphery. Sentience seems definitely a necessary and arguably a sufficient condition for the possession of high moral status (experiments 1 and 2, respectively), whereas the other attributes are arguably necessary but definitely not sufficient (experiments 2 and 1, respectively).

The best way to get a better fix on exactly which traits are prerequisites for moral status is simply to try to explain why they *should* be. Take sentience first. We all agree from personal experience that pain is a bad thing, that no one should have the right to inflict it on us, and consistency (part of any moral system) dictates that we agree not to inflict it on anyone else. Makes sense. But now try to say something comparably compelling about why great reasoning ability or complex language are crucial to moral status. Also, try to do the same with self-consciousness—our awareness of our own existence. (This is another uniquely human attribute commonly invoked in these discussions, but we couldn't isolate it in experiment 1 above because an organism can't have it without having sentience.)

If you accept this challenge, you'll almost certainly go down one of two paths, neither of which will get you very far. First, you may try to establish that self-consciousness, complex language, etc., are the hallmarks of "spirit," the possession of which places us in some special category. This is a perfectly fine thing to believe, but it's hard to *argue* for. It depends much more on religious conviction than on any plausible line of reasoning.

The second path people take in asserting the moral significance of uniquely human attributes is even less successful, because it leads to a booby trap. This is the argument that self-consciousness and reason and language give humans a dimension of suffering that mere animals lack: because we can anticipate pain and death; and because we know that death will represent the end of our consciousness forever; and because we recognize that threats to one citizen may represent a threat to us all—because of all this, the protection of human rights is essential to everyone's peace of mind; the torture or murder of anyone in town, as conveyed to the public via language and then reflected upon at length, makes everyone tremendously fearful. So a robust conception of individual rights is essential for the welfare of a human society in a way that it isn't for, say, the welfare of a chicken society.

Sounds nice, but it amounts to philosophical surrender. To rely completely on this argument is to concede that language, reason, and self-consciousness are morally important *only* to the extent that they magnify suffering or happiness. Pain and pleasure, in other words, are the currency of moral assessment. The several uniquely human attributes may revaluate the currency, but the currency possesses some value with or without them. And many, if not all, nonhuman animals seem to possess the currency in some quantity. So unless you can come up with a non-arbitrary reason for saying that their particular quantities are worthless while our particular quantities are precious, you have to start thinking about animals in a whole new light. This explains why Peter Singer, in *Animal Liberation*, readily admits that the human brain is unique in its ability to thus compound suffering.

Once the jaws of this philosophical trap have closed on the opponents of animal rights, no amount of struggling can free them. Let them insist that language, reason, and self-consciousness *immensely* raise the moral stakes for humans. Let them add, even, that our sheer neurological complexity makes us experience raw pain more profoundly than, say, dogs or even mice do. Grant them, in other words, that in the grand utilitarian calculus, one day of solid suffering by a single human equals one days' suffering by 10,000 laboratory rats. Grant them all of this, and they still lose, because the point is that animals have now been *admitted* to the utilitarian calculus. If it is immoral, as we all believe it is, to walk up to a stranger and inflict 1/10,000 of one day's suffering (nine seconds' worth), then it is equally immoral to walk up and inflict one day's suffering on a single laboratory rat.

Actually, granting animals utilitarian value doesn't technically mean you have to extend individual rights to them. As far as sheer philosophical consistency goes, you can equally well take rights away from humans. You can say: sure, it makes sense to kill

100 baboons to save the life of one human, but it also makes sense to kill a human to save the life of 100 baboons. Whatever you say, though, you have to go one way or the other, letting such equations work either in both directions or in neither. Unless you can create a moral ratchet called "human rights"—and I don't see any way to do it—you have to choose between a planet on which every sentient creature has rights and a planet on which none does.

And of course if no creature on earth has rights, then it can make sense to kill a human not just for the sake of 100 baboons, but for the sake of two humans—or just in the name of the greater good. In other words, the logic used by animals rights activists turns out to play into the hands of the Adolf Hitlers of the world no less than the Albert Schweitzers. In *Darkness at Noon,* when Ivanov describes Stalin's rule as belonging to the school of "vivisection morality." Arthur Koestler is onto something more than good allegory.

Before figuring out whether to follow this logic toward vegetarianism or totalitarianism, let's remove it from the realm of abstraction. Spending an evening watching videotapes supplied by PETA—such as *The Animals Film,* narrated by Julie Christie—is a fairly disturbing experience. This is partly because the people who made it gave it a subtle shrillness that reflects what is most annoying about the animal rights movement. There are man-on-the-street interviews conducted by an obnoxious, self-righteous interrogator demanding to know how people can own dogs and eat Big Macs; there is the assumption that viewers will find the late McDonald's founder Ray Kroc—a seemingly likable guy shown innocently discussing how he settled on the name "McDonald's"—abhorrent; there is a simple-minded anti-capitalist undercurrent (as if factory farmers in socialist countries spent their time giving foot massages to hogs); and there is grating atonal music meant to make the sight of blood more disturbing than it naturally is.

And that's plenty disturbing, thank you. Take, for example, the chickens hung by their feet from a conveyer belt that escorts them through an automatic throat slicing machine—this the culmination of a life spent on the poultry equivalent of a New York subway platform at rush hour. Or consider the deep basketfuls of male chicks, struggling not to smother before they're ground into animal feed. There's also, naturally, the veal: a calf raised in a crate so small that it can't even turn around, much less walk—the better to keep the flesh tender. There are wild furry animals cut almost in half by steel-jawed traps but still conscious. There are rabbits getting noxious chemicals sprayed in their eyes by cosmetics companies.

And these are the animals that *don't* remind you of human beings. Watching these portions of *The Animals Film* is a day at the zoo compared with watching nonhuman primates suffer. If you don't already have a strong sense of identity with chimpanzees, gorillas, and the like—if you doubt that they're capable of crude reasoning, anticipating pain, feeling and expressing deep affection for one another—I suggest you patronize your local zoo (or prison, as animal rights activists would have it) and then get hold of a copy of the ethologist Frans de Waal's two amazing books, *Peacemaking Among Primates* and *Chimpanzee Politics*. The commonly cited fact that chimps share about ninety-eight percent of our genes is misleading, to be sure; a handful of genes affecting the brain's development can make a world of difference. Still, if you can watch a toddler chimp or gorilla for long without wanting to file for adoption, you should seek professional help.

In videotapes that Helen helped steal in 1984 from the University of Pennsylvania's Head Injury Clinical Research Center, anesthetized baboons are strapped down and their heads placed in boxlike vices that are violently snapped sixty degrees sideways by a hydraulic machine. Some of the baboons have what appear to be seizures, some go limp, and none looks very happy. Some of the lab workers—as callous as you'd have to become to do their job, perhaps—stand around and make jokes about it all. It's hard to say how much scientific good came of this, because the scientist in question refuses to talk about it. But watching the tapes, you have to hope that the data were markedly more valuable than what's already available from the study of injured humans. In any event, the experiments were halted after PETA publicized the tapes (though ostensibly for sloppy lab technique, such as occasionally inadequate anesthesia, not because of the violent nature of the experiments).

There are certainly many kinds of animal research that seem justified by any reasonable utilitarian calculus. A case in point is the lab Helen helped set afire at the University of Arizona. Among the researchers whose work was destroyed in the attack is a man named Charles Sterling, who is studying a parasite that causes diarrhea in both animals and humans and kills many children in the Third World every year. There is no way fruitfully to study this parasite in, say, a cell culture, so he uses mice, infecting them with the parasite and thereby inducing a non-lethal spell of diarrhea. (The idea repeated mindlessly by so many animal rights activists—that there's almost always an equally effective non-animal approach to experimentation—is wrong.)

Sterling is one of a handful of workers in this area, and he figures, in over-the-phone, off-the-cuff calculations, that all together they cause around 10,000 to 20,000 mice-weeks of diarrheal discomfort every year. The apparently realistic goal is to find a cure for a disease that kills more than 100,000 children a year. Sounds like a good deal to me. Again, though, the hitch is that to endorse this in a philosophically impeccable way, you have to let go of the concept of human rights, at least as classically conceived.

Then again, human rights isn't what it's classically conceived as being. It isn't some divine law imparted to us from above, or some Platonic truth apprehended through the gift of reason. The idea of individual rights is simply a non-aggression pact among everyone who subscribes to it. It's a deal struck for mutual convenience.

And, actually, it's in some sense a very old deal. A few million years ago, back when human ancestors were not much smarter than chimps, they presumably abided by an implicit and crude concept of individual rights, just as chimps do. Which is to say: life within a troop of, say, fifty or sixty individuals was in practical terms sacred. (Sure, chimps occasionally murder fellow troop members, just as humans do, but this is highly aberrant behavior. Rituals that keep bluster and small-scale aggression from escalating to fatality are well-developed. And when they fail, and death occurs, an entire chimp colony may be solemn and subdued for hours or longer as if in mourning.) At the same time, these prehuman primates were presumably much like chimps in being fairly disdainful of the lives of fellow species-members who didn't belong to the troop. At some point in human history, as troops of fifty became tribes of thousands, the circle of morally protected life grew commensurately. But the circle didn't at first extend to other tribes. Indeed, wide acceptance of the idea that people of all nations have equal moral rights is quite recent.

How did it all happen? In one of Singer's later and less famous books, *The Expanding Circle* (Farrar, Straus, & Giroux, 1981), whose title refers to exactly this process, he writes as if the circle's expansion has been driven almost Platonically, by the "inherently expansionist nature of reasoning." Once people became civilized and started thinking about the logic behind the reciprocal extension of rights to one another, he says, they were on an intellectual "escalator," and there was no turning back. The idea of uniformly applied ethical strictures "emerges because of the social nature of human beings and the requirements of group living, but in the thought of reasoning beings, it takes on a logic of its own which leads to its extension beyond the bounds of the group."

This, alas, is perhaps too rosy a view. The concept of human rights has grown more inclusive largely through raw politics. Had tribes not found it in their interest to band together—sometimes to massacre other tribes—they wouldn't have had to invent the concept of intertribal rights. Necessity was similarly the mother of moral invention in modern societies. Had the suffragists not deftly wielded political clout, men mightn't have seen the logic of giving women the vote. Had the abolition of slavery not acquired political moment in a war that slaughtered millions, slavery might have long persisted.

Certainly in advances of this sort an important role can be played by intellectual persuasion, by sympathy, by empathy. These can fuse with political power and reinforce it. South Africa today exemplifies the mix. President F. W. de Klerk may or may not truly buy the moral logic behind his (relatively) progressive initiatives, but he definitely has felt the accompanying political pressure, ranging from international sanctions to domestic protest and unrest. On the other hand, behind those sanctions has been, among other things, some genuine empathy and some pure moral logic.

The bad news for animals is twofold. First, in all of these cases—women's rights, the abolition of slavery, ending apartheid—a good part of the political momentum comes from the oppressed themselves. Progress in South Africa never would have begun if blacks there hadn't perceived their own dignity and fought for it. Second, in all of these cases, empathy for the oppressed by influential outsiders came because the outsiders could identify with the oppressed—because, after all, they're people, too. With animal rights, in contrast, (1) the oppressed can never by themselves exert leverage; and (2) the outsiders who work on their behalf, belonging as they do to a different species, must be exquisitely, imaginatively compassionate in order to be drawn to the cause. To judge by history, this is not a recipe for success. It may forever remain the case that, when it comes time to sit down and do the moral bargaining, non-human animals, unlike all past downtrodden organisms, don't have much to bring to the table.

Notwithstanding these handicaps, the animal rights movement has made progress. American fur sales are by some accounts down (perhaps more out of fear of social disapproval than out of newfound sympathy). Some cosmetics companies have stopped abusing rabbit's eyes, finding that there are gentler ways to test products. And the university panels that administer federal laboratory regulations—designed to ensure that animal experimentation is worthwhile and not needlessly cruel—are undoubtedly, in the present climate, being at least as scrupulous as they've ever been (however scrupulous that is).

Even I—never quick to bring my deeds into sync with my words—am making minor gains. I hereby vow never again to eat veal. And it's conceivable that the dovetailing of moral concerns and health fears will get me to give up all red meat, among the most (formerly) sentient kind of flesh on the market. Also: no leather couches or leather jackets in my future. Shoes, yes, couches, no; the least we can do is distinguish between the functionally valuable and the frivolous. (Which also means, of course: people who wear fur coats to advertise their social status—which is to say all people who wear fur coats—should indeed, as the Humane Society's ads have it, be ashamed of themselves.) Finally, for what it's worth, I plan to keep intact my lifelong record of never eating pâté de foie gras, the preternaturally enlarged liver of a goose force-fed through a large tube.

But so long as I so much as eat tuna fish and support the use of primates in AIDS research, how can I still endorse the idea of human rights? How can I consider Stalin guilty of a moral crime and not just a utilitarian arithmetic error? One answer would be to admit that my allegiance to human rights isn't philosophical in the pure sense, but pragmatic; I've implicitly signed a non-aggression pact with all other humans, and Stalin violated the pact, which is immoral in this practical sense of the term. But I'd rather answer that, yes, I think moral law should be more than a deal cut among the powerful, but, no, I haven't been any more successful than the next guy in expunging all moral contradictions from my life. I'll try to do what I can.

If there is a half-decent excuse for this particular contradiction, I suppose it is that human civilization is moving in the right direction. Given where our moral thinking was 200, 500, 5000 years ago, we're not doing badly. The expanding circle will never get as big as Singer would like, perhaps, but if it grows even slowly and fitfully, we'll be justified in taking a certain chauvinistic pride in our species.

DOMINION OVER THE EARTH[3]

I recently attended a seminar by one of the leading ethicists in the country. He described the outline of a project in which he has been a participant; in a series of volumes soon to be published, a group of ethicists is attempting to refocus the discussion of ethics. After his presentation, someone asked if there had been any discussion of the treatment of nonhuman animals. The ethicist was somewhat perplexed and intrigued. To his recollection, the issue had never been raised during the several years of discussion.

I was not overly surprised by his answer, but I found it dismaying. Although there is extensive literature on animal rights and cruelty to animals, that particular discourse remains neatly segregated from the main body of ethical discussion in the Western world. A half century ago, Albert Schweitzer wrote that "the time is coming when people will be amazed that the human race was so long before it recognized that thoughtless injury to life is incompatible with real ethics" (*Civilization and Ethics*).

The change of attitude which Schweitzer did foresee is apparently still in our future; at least, any big change among professional ethicists is not yet discernible. However, among ordinary people there has been a slow but steady change over the past two decades.

In making that statement, one is exposed to being considered either a little batty or else a faddish enthusiast for bizarre causes. This "cause" does have its bizarre fringe. Animal rights activists in England and the U.S. have been known to use violence against human beings to save rabbits or mice. No doubt there are misanthropes who die among their hundreds of cats in foul-smelling

[3]Reprint of an article by Gabriel Moran, director of the graduation program of religious education at New York University. *Commonweal.* 114:697-701. D 4 '87. Copyright 1987 by the Commonweal Foundation.

houses. But to see the issue through such aberrations is no more reasonable than to see respect for human life equated with the bombing of abortion clinics.

The argument can be made that, while horses, chimps, seals, or porpoises should not be tortured, there are far more important issues toward which our moral passion should be directed. The tale of human suffering on any nightly news broadcast is already more than we can handle. I think that this attitude of "yes, but" misses the point, which is not simply to add ethical problems to existing ones or to disperse further our limited moral energies. What is at stake is finding an overall moral stance that has deeper roots than either the utilitarian calculus on one side of ethics or the language of individual rights on the other side. The nonhuman animal is a stubborn reminder that morality concerns the reduction of violence, the protection of the vulnerable, the preservation of the life cycle, the union of all things. If the question of nonhuman animals is not part of the reorientation of moral attitude and the reshaping of moral vocabulary, then the "animal rights lobby" may indeed be little more than an ethical sideshow. Thus, a concern with nonhuman animals does not of itself guarantee a new ethical stance, but an obliviousness to the issue strongly suggests that we are still stuck in the rationalism that has dominated modern ethics.

I am very suspicious of the phrase "animal rights." The language of rights is almost the only ethical language that we speak in this country. Thus, when people become sensitive to the issue of "cruelty to animals," the tendency is to extend the concept of rights beyond the human individual. It is assumed that the concept of rights can simply be expanded from blacks to women to gays/lesbians to . . . animals. Granted that the idea of rights is important in modern political systems; the idea has provided important even if limited protection to many human individuals. But crossing the line to the nonhuman world is another kind of step. Indeed, the modern notion of "human rights" was projected *against* the nonhuman world. No sudden flip of the relation will be sufficient for today's problems; a retracing of the path of modern ethics is needed.

Nearly all of modern ethics runs through the person of Immanuel Kant. His primary ethical principle was "to treat each man as an end, never merely as a means." That principle is still quoted widely and solemnly as if it were beyond question. And yet, it is a prescription for ecological disaster. "Man"—the isolated, rational, aggressive male is put at the top of creation. Everything and everyone is put under him. Women and children tend to disappear; even the man's own body should disappear or at least keep quiet. The past is "put behind us" and the future can be whatever "man makes for himself." Nonhuman animals are reduced to "means," that is, to being used in any arbitrary way if it is for the good of "man." Nothing in the world can be called good without qualification, wrote Kant, except the human will.

To his credit, Kant did notice the issue of (nonhuman) animals and agonized a bit over what happens to them in his system. He was impressed by the care which animals give to their young and he thought that they have something to teach us. Nevertheless, animals are not ends in themselves because they are not rational. Thus, if a man shoots his dog, writes Kant, "he does not fail in his duty to the dog, for the dog cannot judge, but the man's act is inhuman and damages in himself that humanity which it is his duty to show toward mankind" (*Lectures on Ethics*).

Kantian ethics is a kind of final abstraction from what was taken to be the Christian view of the world. Kant professed to be giving a philosophical basis for what pious people already believed. However, Nietzsche was to the point in calling Kant "the great delayer," the one who merely postponed the collapse of an ethic that had grown up with modern Western Christianity. Nietzsche did not think that Kant's propped up piety could stand on its own for long, and the twentieth century is proving Nietzsche right on this point. The "man" with his abstract principles is incapable of engaging the bodily suffering that cuts across human and nonhuman worlds. Kantian ethics, centered in agency, deliberately broke with the bodily organism as the basis of ethics.

The chief competitor to Kantian ethics is a utilitarianism based upon the calculation of actual effects in the world of bodily organisms. This line of thinking, most closely associated with Jeremy Bentham, has at least some place for the nonhuman animals. In the nineteenth century, Bentham could write: "The time will come when humanity will extend its mantle over everything which breathes. We have begun by attending to the condition of slaves; we shall finish by softening that of all the animals which assist our labors or supply our wants." The last phrase in this quotation bears noticing; it differentiates Bentham from the likes of Schweitzer. For Bentham, we should improve the condition of

all who "assist our labors or supply our wants." The concern is for
the useful animals; what reigns on high is "man the user." Although some animals are likely to be well treated in such a system,
an ethic centered on possession, use, and consumption is inadequate for today. We need a moral language in which relations
other than usefulness are able to be perceived and appreciated.

It is because of the need for relational language that the question is not "man and animal" but human and nonhuman animals.
The latter phrase already implies the intrinsic relations that constitute bodily life, including human life. The distinctiveness of the
human being emerges in the middle of bodily, animal life not
above it. The question then becomes how do human beings respond to, care for, and love what is not entirely outside themselves. "Animal" is not an alien over which the human has dominion. Especially significant for a moral life is how the human being
treats other animals that appear to be "useless."

Most discussions in this area are still trapped in the language
of "man and animal." Starting from that phrase, animal rights
activists launch attacks on "speciesism," a word coined in the
mid-1970s to refer to an ideology of human superiority. However,
this term can carry a wide range of meaning. At one end, speciesism can refer to the belief that any human desire, however
trivial, outweighs any considerations on the side of the nonhuman. That attitude surely needs criticism and a persuasive case
can be made against it. At the other end, attacks on speciesism can
be made in the name of complete equality among species. The
case for equality seems to me impossible to make; the human
being properly discriminates, for example, between an animal
that obviously suffers pain and organisms that give no evidence of
pain. To walk across the lawn, take a shower, or even breathe is to
assert that *some* human concerns outweigh *some* nonhuman
concerns.

The language of "man and animal" prevents us from asking
the appropriate questions about reducing violence to all living
things. When the question is "man and animal," and when some
competition in this world is inevitable, then the issue of superiority is immediately clear. The vast majority of "men" are going to
come down on the side of the "man's" superiority; it is inconceiva-
ble that they could do otherwise. If, however, one speaks of
human and nonhuman animals, then what first surfaces are the
various forms of interrelation and interdependence. One asks

how to share, how to understand, how to reach a harmony. Within that context, one has to ask realistically about which human concerns are more important than others; one has to ask about the weighing of a variety of important concerns in a total ecological system; one has to accept competition and conflict as a regular fact of life, not just an invention of human civilization. But conflict does not have to mean indiscriminate violence; animals, including the human kind, need ways to negotiate their conflicts. Obviously, the humans are supposed to use their intelligence as part of the process of negotiation: intelligence situated in the middle of bodily life.

Some of these decisions should be morally clear. The human need for food outweighs the apple's proclivity to stay on the tree as long as possible. The human desire for mink coats does not outweigh the sufferings of millions of animals that die excruciatingly painful deaths. Between such extremes as these, human beings have to make fallible and always biased decisions about what lives and what dies. It is not simply a question of whether "man" is or is not superior to the animal; the question concerns the thousands of gradations of importance in the interrelation of living beings. People who accept the language of "man" vs. "animal" and then try to defend the animal are trapped in a futile rebellion. A combination of hidden paternalism and sentimentalism is not going to make the world safe for women, children, men, and nonhuman animals.

Nearly all of the major religions have been especially concerned with the treatment of nonhuman animals. Both Eastern and Western religions situate the human being at the center of a matrix of living beings. The Jewish-Christian tradition begins with a Creator who brings into existence a hierarchy of things. Each thing is pronounced good, with the living things having a special dignity that gives witness to the "living God." In contrast to the two competing systems of modern ethics in which the good is the object of human desire, Jewish and Christian religions recognize the good to be whatever exists, whatever receives existence from the hand of God.

In the course of history, Jewish and Christian religions seemed to jump too quickly from the general proposition that "everything is good" to the central affirmation that "man is good." Other animals did not receive the affirmation that they deserved. The separating out of the rational, aggressive, controlling "man," has been the glory but also the danger in Western religion. The feminist and ecological movements have frequently regarded Christianity as the enemy. In comparison to Buddhist or Native American religions, Western Christianity has often been deficient in recognizing the sacredness of each living thing. The nonhuman animals tended to get absorbed into an abstraction called nature. With its stress on "man's dominion over the earth," Christianity helped prepare the way for the project of seventeenth-century science: "Man will put nature to the rack and demand answers" (F. Bacon).

With the Kantian ethic having come to such dominance in the nineteenth century, we find it difficult to remember any other way of thinking. In earlier periods of Christianity, there were at least other strands. While Thomas Aquinas was not entirely opposed to Kant on this point, one can perceive some differences, such as in this passage from the *Summa Theologicae:* "Since it happens that even irrational animals are sensible to pain, it is possible for the affection of pity to arise in a man with regard to the sufferings of animals. Now it is evident that if a man practices a pitiful affection for animals, he is all the most disposed to take pity on his fellow man."

At least Aquinas in this passage talks about the relation of irrational animals and the other (that is, human) animals, about the need for practicing a pitiful affection for (nonhuman) animals, and about the fact that such affection, far from being in opposition to care for human beings, is joined to such care. The Catholic church often issued warnings against societies for the protection of animals. The reason seems to be the assumption that the human being has a fixed amount of care to dispose of so that any care for nonhumans diminishes care for humans. To Aquinas, "it is evident" that the opposite is the case.

The right wing of contemporary Christianity wishes to have no blurring of the line between "animal" and "man." The result is a furious attack on Darwin and evolution. What is typically defended in "creation science" is the scientific picture of the seventeenth and eighteenth centuries. This science provided the background for Kantian ethics, that is, animals are things for use, man is mind and soul. While Darwin's theory, when it was extended into social policy, was often used in brutalizing ways, his idea of evolution attempted to restore a sense of unity and dignity to the entire realm of life. The theory of evolution does not "degrade man to the level of the beast"; rather, it affirms life in all of its various forms placing men and women at the responsible center of the whole process.

Such a reintegration does not eliminate all distinctions of moral worth. On the contrary, instead of drawing a single line between what is valuable and what is not, we need numerous moral distinctions. Eastern religions or the life mysticism of a Schweitzer do not offer a perfect model because there is still too much reliance on a single line dividing "life" and everything else. What is respected and sometimes almost deified is "nature" or "life." But moral worth, it seems to me, lies not in such generalized abstractions, but in the concrete reality of living organisms themselves. Surely some moral distinctions have to be made in the continuum of creation; there must exist some reasonable differentiation between dolphins and mosquitoes, redwoods and crabgrass.

At one end of the organic spectrum is the highly complex animal. The animals that humans recognize as most similar to themselves have something akin to personality. The individual in these species asserts its right to exist and to develop toward its own fulfillment. Christopher Lasch, in his book *The Minimal Self* . . . writes: "If men were moved solely by impulse and self-interest, they would be content like other animals, simply to survive. Nature knows no will-to-power, only a will-to-live." Lasch may be right about what "nature knows," but he is wrong about individual nonhuman animals in nature who, like the human kind, assert their preferences and delight in being themselves. Has Lasch never tried to get a cat off his lap or watched chimpanzees at play?

At the other end of the spectrum it is not apparent that the individual has the same value—which is not to say that it is valueless. If a cockroach can reproduce 400,000 offspring, it is difficult to believe that it has a special parental feeling for each of its progeny. If an organism's life expectancy is by human measuring a single day, can it have a sense of historical development toward maturity? Perhaps. But "nature" certainly seems to be saying something different at this end of the spectrum. The existing reality even here is an individual not a general life force. In regard to these life forms, however, human beings must realistically attend to the protection of the species rather than every individual of the species. A person who takes pleasure or spends a lot of time in killing bugs may be morally obtuse; but a person who suffers guilt or spends much time in trying to avoid the killing of a single bug may also be misdirecting his or her moral concern.

What we should be morally concerned about in this country is the continuing destruction of whole species. In classical and medieval times, philosophers considered it important that the whole chain of being be complete. The theologians held that once God had decided to create, then He had to create every kind of thing. Their science may have been primitive but perhaps their moral sense was correct. At least, contemporary humans ought to consider as morally important the permanent destruction of species, which human beings had no part in creating and which had been here for hundreds of thousands of years. The Eastern respect for life and Western scientific detail need finally to be combined so that we can protect in effective ways the ecological texture of life.

Returning to the other end of the spectrum, we can see that the protection of complex nonhuman animals also involves a sense of moral and aesthetic wholeness. But it also involves a refocusing of the question upon the individual's well being. As we should not unnecessarily inflict pain upon a human being, so a dog or a cow or a deer merits our concern not to impose pain on the basis of human whim. Of course, the meaning of "necessary pain" raises difficult questions.

One can distinguish today three areas of debate over the treatment of nonhuman animals: cosmetics, experimentation, and food.

Starting with the first and easiest, one can say simply that the use of animals for cosmetic purposes ought to be banned. At an earlier period of human history, the use of an animal's fur for keeping a person alive may have been justifiable. The human hunter and the nonhuman animal may have confronted one another at the level of survival. Today, however, the fur industry uses methods that are barbaric in order to produce a product that is unnecessary.

Experimentation is a more complicated area. Some people argue for a complete ban on the use of nonhuman animals in the laboratory. I do not see that position as morally necessary. What we could hope for, however, is increasing openness about what is being done and how. For example, the forced feeding of toxic substances to nonhuman animals in order to see if 50 percent of them die is a form of protecting human life that is out of proportion to the good being sought. In contrast, the use of some animals in developing a serum to stop an epidemic is a position that could gain support from Eastern religions as well as Western science. There remain complicated questions about how animals are obtained for laboratories, how they are kept in captivity, and how they are actually used. Sensitive experimenters and well enforced legal codes could reduce the amount of pain that lab animals suffer.

Finally, there is food. A total ban on animals for food is not likely to happen although there has been a dramatic shift away from a red meat diet. Health concern more than the moral treatment of nonhuman animals appears to be the reason, but healthy diet also has its proper place in morality. The argument of this essay does not necessarily lead to vegetarianism. But at the least it does lead to questioning how meat is produced and whether we need further radical changes in the direction of deriving protein from nonanimal sources. Most of us are completely sheltered from the harsh reality between the animal grazing contentedly in a field and the piece of steak on our plate. Of course, the animal might not have had existence at all if it were not being grown for food and, furthermore, scientific methods can lessen pain as well as mass produce it. But I wonder if people were to see at close range how milk-fed calves live in motionless and darkened existence, whether the same people would order veal marsala in a restaurant. Perhaps they still would do so, but their sensitivity to allowing excruciating animal existence for unnecessary human luxury is not given the chance to be tested.

Vegetarians provide a witness of protest against the rest of the meat-eating culture. That witness needs the cooperation of those who wish to reform eating patterns in less radical ways. Animals can be cultivated for food that form a more efficient part of the ecological cycle. A continued reduction in the amount of meat would be good for human health as well as nonhuman discomfort. A shift toward eating more fish has been occurring. As this shift continues, it is crucially important that natural cycles of fish life in the ocean not be destroyed. Life on earth does involve some competition and conflict; the human being in particular cannot avoid inflicting some pain. However, they can today combine scientific knowledge and moral sensitivity so as to lessen unnecessary pain to all the animals. The humans have an appropriate predilection for the human animal but their feeling for the defenseless nonhuman animal is a good test of their resistance to violence everywhere.

ANIMAL LIB[4]

The animal-rights movement raises questions about more than animals. Ultimately, it raises the question of whether a secular society can make sense of itself.

An image: I am 11 years old, and on a bright, spring day I stand on the banks of an irrigation ditch that runs near my school. Someone has caught a frog, and two boys are taking turns throwing their pocket knives at it. I can catch only occasional glimpses of the frog through the legs of my peers, who are crowding around, eager to see.

After many tries, a knife finds its target, and the crowd lets out an admiring groan. I press closer. The frog, split open, is leaking its guts. Still living, it scrabbles weakly in the dust. I turn away feeling sick and guilty. I know without a shadow of a doubt that what I have seen is wrong. This should never be done to a frog.

Another image: I am 31 years old, and on another bright, spring day I watch a goat die. I am in Kenya, and as is traditional in East African celebrations, a goat is being slaughtered for a barbecue. I have eaten meat right out of the cellophane all my life, but I have never seen a mammal die. So I stand with a huddle of African friends, watching the deed with horrified fascination. It is done quickly, without cruelty. The neck is slit and blood spurts out. The goat bleats, struggles, and then lies still. It is gutted, skinned, cut apart. Nothing is wasted. The intestines are cooked; the head goes into a pot for soup. The meat, even after it is cut into pieces for the grill, has a habit of twitching.

I feel a little shaken by what I have seen. I do not feel ashamed, but I do feel solemn. It is not so light a thing to take an animal's life.

---

[4]Reprint of an article by staff writer Tim Stafford. *Christianity Today.* 34:18+. Je 18 '90. Copyright 1990 by Christianity Today, Inc. Reprinted by permission.

Confronting Speciesism

Almost everyone would accept what my 11-year-old mind concluded about the needless death of a frog: It was wrong.

About the death of the goat, not all would agree. Most people have thought that as long as the goat was killed for food, and did not suffer more than necessary, its killing was justified. A persistent minority, however, has questioned our right to use animals for our own ends, as though they were merely "things."

Despite such differences of opinion, virtually all Western people have worked from the Christian premise that human beings were set apart by God for a special purpose and for special responsibilities. We are worth more than the animals, and we must act better than animals—so we have believed. Those who wanted to protect animals from suffering worked from this assumption, as did those who justified using and eating animals.

But no more. Today, the most visible animal-rights activists speak out against the belief that humankind has been put in charge of creation. This presumption, they claim, has led to the overwhelming slavery and abuse that animals suffer. They scoff at the Christian requirement that we treat animals kindly. It is, they say, like the requirement that slaveowners treat their slaves kindly. The activists' goal is to set the animals free—free from all human control and domination.

"Humane treatment is simply sentimental, sympathetic patronage," says Michael W. Fox, a veterinarian who directs the Center for the Respect of Life and Environment at the Humane Society of the United States.

Tom Regan, another well-known activist, puts it this way: "The animal-rights philosophy is abolitionist rather than reformist. It's not better cages we work for, but empty cages." Gary Francione, a law professor who litigates animal-rights cases, would not allow an animal to suffer even if the research led to a cancer cure: "I don't believe it is morally permissible to exploit weaker beings even if we derive benefits."

In a *Harper's* magazine forum on the morality of animal experimentation, the theoretical possibility of implanting a pig's heart to save a human baby's life was raised. One animal-rights activist, who is sternly against such a possibility, said that the baby's parents should be made to care about the pig. When another participant exclaimed, "I don't want to change [the parent's] reaction. I want human beings to care about babies," Ingrid

Newkirk, head of People for the Ethical Treatment of Animals, retorted, "Like racism or sexism, that remark is pure speciesism."

Speciesism, a term invented in Peter Singer's foundational text, *Animal Liberation,* is the allegedly bigoted contention that human beings are more important than other animals. "It can no longer be maintained by anyone but a religious fanatic that man is the special darling of the universe," Singer wrote, "or that other animals were created to provide us with food, or that we have divine authority over them, and divine permission to kill them."

That makes animal rights one of the first social movements to claim an explicitly non-Christian point of view. Not all its members share this ideology, but the most publicized leaders speak against long-held Christian assumptions. Michael Fox, quoted in *The Washingtonian,* put it succinctly: "There are no clear distinctions between us and animals. Animals communicate, animals have emotions, animals can think. Some thinkers believe that the human soul is different because we are immortal, and that just becomes completely absurd." Humane Society literature, according to writer Katie McCabe, has claimed since 1980 that "there is no rational basis for maintaining a moral distinction between the treatment of humans and other animals."

Sputtering and Fuming

It is tempting to focus on the abrupt twists and turns in the logic of animal-rights activists. They point to science's inability to document absolute differences between human and beast. But this hardly suggests that we should treat animals well. It should be instructive to note that mere animals eat each other: that is, whales eat seals, seals eat fish, all without evident taint of "speciesism." Clearly, to animal-rights activists, human beings are special—special in their responsibility to treat animals better than many animals treat each other. The animal-rights movement would like to raise animals to the moral status of humans. It would be just as *logical* to lower humans to the moral status of animals.

But why hold animal-rights activists to a higher standard of logic than their opponents? The philosophy of animal rights does not seem coherent, but as a number of thinkers have noted, a secular philosophy of human rights has yet to prove coherent, either.

This is quite noticeable in the back-and-forth between animal-rights activists and the scientists, government officials, and journalists who confront them. Both sides argue fervently from a position firmly planted in the air. The activists ask: What gives humankind the right to decide an animal's fate? Why should a monkey lose its life to save a child? In response, the sages of our society sputter and fume.

Scientists have been amazed and outraged as the protests of what they regard as a lunatic fringe have disturbed the sanctity of their laboratories. Although typically not philosophically inclined, scientists do have a solemn sense of purpose in what they do. This gets expressed in various ways. At the high end is the philosophical: We are pursuing the truth, they say. At the low end is the pragmatic: We are saving lives through medicine.

It is at the low end that scientists usually try to meet the animal-rights activists. John Kaplan, writing in *Science*, suggests that scientists show photos of "human burn victims or of quadriplegics to offset the pathetic pictures of the animals used in the research." He assumes that people will favor the suffering of animals over the suffering of human beings, and he is probably right about that.

But as far as the activists are concerned, this begs the question. What right have we to make an animal suffer in our place? We would not consider it right to treat another human being that way. Why an animal? What makes us think we are so special?

Ironically, the biologist proclaiming urgently that every delay in their experiments may cost human lives are members of the discipline that has been at pains to show there is no dramatic difference between humans and other animals, that different species are merely different products of evolution. By their own criteria, one is not "better" than another.

But now scientists have made a different discovery: In their heart of hearts they believe that human beings are morally different from animals. Only they cannot say why they think so. They can only sputter with outrage that anyone would put a human being on the same level as a pig.

Dangerous Thinking

A 1988 *Newsweek* cover story ended with these remarks on vivisection:

The question is whether the practical benefits of vivisection constitute a moral justification for it. If mankind's interest in finding a better treatment for AIDS doesn't justify conducting lethal experiments on individual humans, an ethicist might ask, why does it justify performing them on monkeys? Why doesn't a monkey deserve moral consideration? What is the relevant difference between a human subject and an animal subject?

To reply that the human is human and the animal isn't only begs the question. . . .

Another possible answer is that we humans enjoy certain God-given prerogatives. We are, after all, the only creatures the Bible says were made in God's image. . . .

It may be a difference, but it's not an empirical, observable one. It has to be taken on faith. . . .

Maybe there is no reasoned moral justification . . . Whatever the answer, scientists can no longer afford to pretend that their critics' moral concerns are frivolous. Profound questions are being raised, and ignoring them won't make them go away.

On that uncertain note, the long article ended. On a similar note, a 1990 *New Republic* article by Robert Wright [also in this compilation. See page 20.] essentially accepted the argument that no moral distinction can be made between animals and humans. The belief that humans are in a special category, wrote Wright, "is a perfectly fine thing to believe, but it's hard to argue for. It depends much more on religious conviction than on any plausible line of reasoning." And of course, Wright assumed, religious conviction was ruled out of reasonable discussion.

Unfortunately, Wright also showed where his assumptions can lead: "Human rights . . . isn't some divine law imparted to us from above, or some Platonic truth apprehended through the gift of reason. The idea of individual rights is simply a non-aggression pact. . . . It's a deal struck for mutual convenience."

Wright showed the danger of excluding religion from questions that are inherently religious. Investigating animal rights through pure logic, without revelation, can easily turn against human rights, and ultimately against animals. If human rights are merely "a deal struck for mutual convenience," then anybody who doesn't buy into the deal (Stalin, say) is morally free to go his or her own way. And of course it makes no sense at all to extend the deal to animals, whose protection and care is certainly not a matter of mutual convenience. Humans will only care for animals if they believe that it is a calling, not a "deal."

As Richard John Neuhaus has put it, "The campaign against 'speciesism' is a campaign against the singularity of human dignity and, therefore, of human responsibility . . . . The hope for a more humane world, including the more humane treatment of animals, is premised upon what they deny."

Opponents of animal-rights activists also sometimes fall into logic that is inherently dangerous. Why should medical researchers sacrifice animals for human welfare? Journalist Katie McCabe suggests an answer of sorts in her *Washingtonian* exposé of animal-rights activists, "Beyond Cruelty." She points out that the debate "has been framed . . . as everything but what it really is—a moral argument that penetrates to the definition of humanity." She then quotes businessman Richard Kelly: The debate "is not an argument that philosophy or religion or even science can solve. . . . In the end, human beings and their needs are the only argument that matters."

This is a kind of "defending my family" argument. It goes, "I don't know who's better, them or us. But I know that if I have to choose, I'm fighting for us." This is pure speciesism, if you please. Anything that enhances, protects, or increases the joy of the human race is good. Why? Because it's my team. This is a form of humanism that justifies animal experiments, but a great deal more—too much more. There is no limit to what it will justify in the name of the human race.

What we see through the lens of this controversy is a society that has lost faith in the religious view it was built on and has nothing suitable to put in its place. The religious sentiments continue—on the part of animal-rights activists, the sympathy for animal suffering, and on the part of scientists, the belief in human pre-eminence—but the sentiments have lost their foundation. When someone challenges them, the response is the agitated indignation of people who are sure they are doing the right thing, though they cannot say why. Animal-rights activists cannot articulate why they care about the death of a frog, or the death of a child. Nor can scientists say why they would kill a frog to save a child. They argue from feeling—a feeling that banks on thousands of years of a faith in which they no longer believe.

The Spectrum of Christian Thought

Despite all efforts to rule religion out, the debate over animal rights remains inherently and fundamentally religious. That is not to say, however, that religion offers only one answer. Hinduism, for example, has its own view, to which some animal-rights activists are attracted. And within Christianity there is room for tremendous differences—room for the chicken farmer viewing his birds as meat-making machines, as well as for Saint Francis preaching sermons to them.

The chicken farmer claims familiar scriptural supports. According to his view, God intended animals to serve human ends, and it is no cruelty to use them for their created purpose. Genesis 1 describes how humankind was charged with ruling "over the fish of the sea and the birds of the air . . . and over all the creatures that move along the ground" (v. 26, NIV). Genesis 9:3, furthermore, records how God gave all living creatures to Noah and his family for food. Biblical people—including Jesus—were flesh eaters. They were also animal users—shepherds and fishermen and dirt farmers who used animals to plow and thresh. The Bible treats this as normal.

Another view of animals is also explicit in the Bible, however, and gives a different (though not necessarily contradictory) perspective. It is presented most vividly in Psalm 104. There, animals find their niche in creation alongside humanity, not beneath it. Some animals are of no use to humankind—may even be hazardous to human persons. Lions "seek their food from God" and go to bed when humans go out to work. In the sea can be found "leviathan, which you formed to frolic there" (Ps. 104:26, NIV). Animals, however useful they are to humankind, are supremely valuable to God, who made them in their uniqueness for his own purposes.

As Karl Barth described creation, humankind "is not set up as lord over the earth, but as lord on the earth which is already furnished with these creatures. Animals and plants do not belong to him; they and the whole earth can belong only to God." Thus our responsibility is not to use the living creatures of the earth for our own purposes, but to rule the earth in such a way as to ensure that all God's creatures are able to fulfill his purposes. In some cases—the whale, the lion—that surely means leaving them to be themselves.

Between these two emphases—the instrumental and the ecological—there are many possibilities. On one side are the pragmatic, workaday realities of society as we know it. By this, certain animals are good for food, for wool, for experiments. If this good involves some bad—some unavoidable pain, for example—that is how life often is on a fallen planet, a tradeoff between good and bad, nurture and suffering.

On the other side is the good of the peaceable kingdom, where the lion will lie down with the lamb, and no one will hurt or destroy. So it was in Eden, so it will be in the end—and so we ought to try to make it today.

What both ends of the Christian spectrum share is as important as their differences. Both sides believe that humanity has a unique calling, and that our relationship to animals must be worked out within that calling. Christians do not share the modern uncertainty about what on earth we are here for, an uncertainty that adds a wild and flailing quality to secularized debates over animal rights.

A More Peaceable Kingdom

The animal-rights movement would like to change the world dramatically. Some changes can be made fairly painlessly. We could do without furs, for instance. At some level, though, there is little doubt that animal rights are in conflict with human need. Nearly all scientists say, for instance, that medical research requires animal experimentation. Give it up, and you just as surely give up cures for a thousand diseases. It is difficult to imagine our society giving those up without stronger reasons than animal-rights activists have so far offered.

More likely, a goal disdained by activists will be fulfilled: Our society will try to be kinder to animals, even as it uses them and eats them.

The industrialization of food production, global pollution, and the crowding out of wilderness bring new questions about our treatment of animals. Today lions can go their independent way only if we set aside space for them to do so. Whales will survive to frolic only as we restrain our tendency to use them for our ends. God made them; we can now unmake them. One hopes that the animal-rights movement will prod our society to think seriously about such issues.

We can share another hope: Perhaps if activists keep asking questions, they will lead us to the realization that no society can be purely irreligious. We must, when asked for the reasons behind our commitments, be able to say more than "science." Scientists who have discovered so many wonderful secrets of the universe have yet to discover an ethic. Science has its ethical commitments, but they are inherited, assumed.

At our society's center, increasingly, is confusion. Having shed

Christianity, we have no framework for thinking about ecology, suffering, life, and death—whether for animals or for humans. This void will be filled, perhaps with a resurgence of Christian humanism, or perhaps with something else. No lasting society is truly and fully pluralistic, in the sense of not having any core beliefs. If animal-rights activists accidentally bring this point home, they may do more for humans than they do for animals.

II. ANIMALS IN RESEARCH

EDITOR'S INTRODUCTION

No issue in the animal-rights agenda is as bitterly contested as the question of scientific experiments on animals, for this is where the values of humans are most in conflict. In order to save ourselves from suffering, we must gain scientific knowledge, but in order to gain that knowledge, we must cause animals to suffer. The pain and isolation endured by laboratory animals—an estimated 20 million each year in the United States alone—enrages animal advocates, whether it is caused for frivolous reasons (testing a new mascara) or for serious ones (seeking a cure for juvenile diabetes). Scientists, who believe that they are acting out of compassion for humanity, are upset by their portrayal as torturers with no motive other than profit. The complexities of the situation are surveyed in the first article in this section, "Of Pain and Progress," by Geoffrey Cowley.

The orthodox animal-rights position on the use of sentient animals in research is given in the second article by Steven Siegel, the founder of Trans-Species Unlimited (now known as the Animal Rights Movement). His argument has two main points: first, animal research is useless because of the physical and psychological differences between humans and animals; second, it is in any case unjust to subject one group of creatures to pain and misery merely to serve the interests of a more powerful group.

Various rebuttals to this position are given in the next three selections. The first, by Frankie L. Trull, a prominent spokeswoman for medical researchers, recounts stories of people who were saved from catastrophic illness by treatments developed through animal research. The next is a condensation of a position paper prepared by the American Medical Association. The authors, in addition to listing dozens of medical advances achieved with the help of animal studies, reject on scientific grounds the claims of animal advocates that the majority of experiments are unnecessary. The same argument is delivered in more personal and dramatic terms by pediatrician Ron Karpati in his article "A Scientist: 'I Am the Enemy.'"

49

Charges and rebuttals aside, economic factors alone have begun to encourage medical researchers to find ways of reducing their use of animals. It is increasingly costly to purchase specially bred laboratory animals or to capture animals from the wild and to feed and maintain them. In the sixth selection, researchers Alan M. Goldberg and John M. Frazier describe how the use of cultured liver cells and egg membranes is slowly replacing such traditional methods as the Draize test, in which substances are evaluated by the damage they cause to the eyes of live, unanesthetized rabbits.

The thorniest moral dilemma in medical research is the use of primates—chimpanzees, gorillas, and baboons. Because they are so closely related to humans, they make ideal subjects for a variety of experiments. But for the same reason, to many people their suffering seems particularly terrible. The final selection, "A Plea for the Chimps," by the famous primatologist Jane Goodall, is an account of her campaign to encourage laboratories to meet the social and psychological needs of the primates whose lives are in their control.

OF PAIN AND PROGRESS[1]

For 14 years, Michiko Okamoto heard nothing but praise for the medical experiments she performed on animals. By force-feeding barbiturates to groups of cats for periods of several weeks, then cutting off their supplies, the Cornell University pharmacologist learned a lot about the dynamics of addiction and withdrawal. She showed that the moderate drug doses prescribed by physicians can, over time, be as physically addictive as the fixes sold on the street. And she explained why addicts die from overdoses even after their bodies have grown tolerant of particular drugs. Okamoto's work won numerous grants from the National Institute on Drug Abuse (NIDA) and her findings are cited in standard medical texts. According to Keith Killam, a professor of pharmacology at the University of California, Davis, the cat experiments are "a shining, crystal example of how to do science."

[1]Reprint of an article by Geoffrey Cowley and others. From *Newsweek*, 114:12-3, D 26 '88. Copyright © 1988 by Newsweek, Inc. All rights reserved. Reprinted by permission.

Steve Siegel of Trans-Species Unlimited, a Pennsylvania-based animal-rights group, calls them "the worst of the worst." Last year Siegel's group mounted a massive campaign against Okamoto. It printed brochures describing, in her own words, how her cats would stand "trembling [and] salivating" after she suddenly stopped pumping drugs into their stomachs—how they would hiss at imagined tormentors or collapse and die "during or soon after periods of continuous convulsive activity." For four months Trans-Species' supporters picketed Okamoto's laboratory and barraged her with phone calls. Cornell and NIDA officials received more than 10,000 letters condemning the experiments.

This fall [1988], after making a statement that was widely, if mistakenly, viewed as a promise to stop the cat studies, Cornell and Okamoto surrendered. In an unprecedented gesture, they wrote NIDA to say they would forfeit a new $530,000 three-year research grant.

It was, depending on your perspective, a moral victory for abused and innocent creatures or a defeat for science and medicine. Either way, the case of the Cornell cats was just the latest example of America's growing preoccupation with the moral status of animals. Scholars say more has been written on the subject in the past 12 years than in the previous 3,000. And grassroots organizations are proliferating wildly. Just 15 years ago, talk of animal welfare was pretty well confined to the humane societies. Today there are some 7,000 animal-protection groups in the United States, with combined memberships of 10 million and total budgets of some $50 million. Says Carol Burnett, spokeswoman for the Washington-based group People for the Ethical Treatment of Animals: "We're really gaining steam."

That's not to say everybody's riding the same train. The activists' demands range from securing better lab conditions to setting all animals free, and their tactics range from letter writing to burglary. Yet they've become a potent collective presence. Animal advocates have sponsored numerous local ballot initiatives to regulate the treatment of farm animals, or ban the use of animals in product-safety tests, or exempt school kids from mandatory dissection lessons. They've declared war on the fur industry, agitated against particular scientists, as in the Cornell case, and organized to block construction of new animal-research facilities. At Stanford University, plans for a new $18 million animal lab were held up for more than a year when the Palo Alto Humane Society opposed the project before the county board of supervisors. Construction is now under way, but the delay cost the university more than $2 million.

There has been civil disobedience, too—even violence. Just last month, a woman affiliated with the animal-rights cause was arrested outside the United States Surgical Corp. in Norwalk, Conn., and charged with planting a radio-controlled pipe bomb near the company chairman's parking place. Fires and break-ins, many of them linked to the militant Animal Liberation Front, have caused millions of dollars' worth of damage at labs around the country. The fear of such incidents is fast turning research centers into bunkers. After two bomb threats and at least five attempted break-ins, officials at Emory University's Yerkes Regional Primate Research Center recently spent hundreds of thousands of dollars on new alarms and electronic locks. Other institutions, including Harvard Medical School, have taken similar steps.

In short, the debate over animal rights is forcing basic changes in the way universities, corporations and government agencies do business. More than that, it's prompting a reconsideration of mankind's place in the web of life. As the political scientist Walter Truett Anderson observes in his recent book "To Govern Evolution," the cause of animal rights is not just a passing fancy. It is a "principled attempt to redefine some of our most basic concepts about the nature of political rights and obligations."

Immense Benefits

The number of creatures used in research, education and product testing each year is indeed staggering. Though estimates run as high as 100 million, federal agencies place the total at 17 million to 22 million—a figure that includes some 50,000 cats, 61,000 primates, 180,000 dogs, 554,000 rabbits and millions of mice and rats (which fill 80 to 90 percent of the demand).

The killing is not without purpose; it has immense practical benefits. Animal models have advanced the study of such diseases as cancer, diabetes and alcoholism and yielded lifesaving treatments for everything from heart disease to manic-depressive illness. Vaccines developed through animal research have virtually wiped out diseases like smallpox and polio. "Every surgical technique was tried first in animals," says Frankie Trull, executive director of the Foundation for Biomedical Research. "Every drug anybody takes was tried first in animals."

By the same token, today's animal research may lead to better medicine in the future. Right now, researchers at the University of California School of Medicine, Davis, are infecting Asian rhesus monkeys with the simian AIDS virus, to see whether early treatment with the drug AZT will keep them from developing symptoms. Because the monkeys normally get sick within 10 months of infection—not the three to five years common in humans—the study will determine quickly whether the same treatment might save human lives.

At Houston's Baylor College of Medicine, Glen Martin and Brenda Lonsbury-Martin are using rabbits to study the hearing loss caused by environmental noise. By attaching small speakers to a rabbit's ears, the researchers can give the animal a large daily dose of noise resembling that of a blow-dryer or a factory or a construction site, and plot its effect. Knowing exactly how particular kinds of noise affect hearing would, of course, help us avoid the most dangerous ones. It might also suggest strategies for cleaning up the auditory environment.

At Emory University's Yerkes center, other researchers are performing cataract surgery on healthy baby rhesus monkeys, hoping to devise better postsurgical therapies for the human children who undergo the operation. After performing the surgery, neurobiologist Ronald Boothe and his colleagues give different monkeys slightly different rehabilitative treatments, all of which involve placing an opaque contact lens over the good eye and a corrective lens in the wounded eye. After a year of therapy, the researchers kill the animals and dissect their brains to see which treatment has promoted the most development within the visual cortex. "We have kids being born who are going to go blind without this research," Boothe says. "By me doing this research, we can prevent them from going blind. Most people, given that choice, will think it's justified.

Moral Costs

If the issue were that simple, animal experimentation might never have become so controversial. But as the philosopher Peter Singer demonstrated in 1975, it's not. In a book called "Animal Liberation," Singer questioned the assumption that securing practical benefits for mankind automatically justifies experimentation on other animals. Indeed, he condemned that notion as "a form of prejudice no less objectionable than prejudice about a person's race or sex," and he urged that we "consider our attitudes from the point of view of those who suffer by them."

To provide that perspective Singer had only to recount what

scientists themselves had written in mainstream professional journals. In a chapter titled "Tools for Research," he sampled the recent literature from such diverse fields as toxicology and psychology, and it wasn't easy reading. He described standard government tests in which beagles were fed pesticides or bombarded with radiation until they lay bleeding from the mouth and anus. And he recounted numerous experiments in which psychologists subjected intelligent animals to fear or hopelessness or "psychological death" in crude attempts to analyze these emotional states.

In a 1972 paper in the Journal of Comparative and Physiological Psychology, for example, researchers at the Primate Research Center in Madison, Wis., described placing baby monkeys alone in a stainless-steel tank for periods of up to 45 days. They wanted to see whether confinement in this "well of despair" would cause lasting psychological damage. It did. The animals exhibited what the researchers termed "severe and persistent psychopathological behavior of a depressive nature." But the paper stressed the preliminary nature of this finding, saying further studies were needed to determine whether the symptoms could be "traced specifically to variables such as chamber shape, chamber size, duration of confinement [or] age at time of confinement." (No such experiments have been conducted at the Madison center since 1974.)

In other papers, the same scientists described efforts to gauge the effects of child abuse on young monkeys. In one experiment they designed mechanical surrogate mothers who would eject sharp brass spikes as the youngsters hugged them. The experience seemed to have no serious effect; the infants "simply waited until the spikes receded and then returned and clung to the mother." So, in a refinement of the experiment, the researchers forcibly impregnated females who had been driven mad through social isolation, and turned them loose on their own offspring. "One of [the mothers'] favorite tricks," they wrote, "was to crush the infant's skull with their teeth."

These programs were not mere atrocities, Singer argued. They were examples of scientists "doing what they were trained to do, and what thousands of their colleagues do." The peer-reviewed journals were brimming with similar stories. Researchers studying how punishment affects learning suspended dogs in hammocks and administered shocks through electrodes taped to their paws. Other investigators, curious to know how various drugs would affect a subject's responsiveness to punishment, implanted electrodes near pigeons' genitals, gave them drugs, then shocked them every time they pecked keys they'd learned to associated with food.

If Singer's work gave birth to a new social movement, a young activist named Alex Pacheco helped it grow. Pacheco, who was moved by Singer's book to help organize the group People for the Ethical Treatment of Animals (PETA), took a job in 1981 as a lab assistant at the Institute for Behavioral Research in Silver Spring, Md. Once he had his own keys, he was able to spend several months sneaking in at night to document the mistreatment of 17 monkeys being used in a study of spinal cord injury. Researchers had severed nerves to the monkeys' arms and were testing their ability to use the crippled limbs by shocking the animals when they failed. Pacheco's widely publicized photographs showed monkeys covered with open, infected wounds. Some had chewed the ends off their fingers. All were confined to filth-encrusted cages just a foot and a half wide.

Steady Progress

Since then, similarly troubling conditions have come to light at a number of respected research centers. Yet all parties seem to agree that the general situation has improved markedly since 1980. The number of animals destroyed in experiments, however staggering, has declined steadily as researchers have come up with cheaper and more humane alternatives, such as cell cultures and computer models. And scientists using live animals have, as a general rule, become more conscientious and more accountable. "A lot of people are learning, a lot are trying," says Ingrid Newkirk, the British-born activist who founded PETA with Alex Pacheco eight years ago.

One of the first tangible changes came about in 1985, when Congress passed a series of amendments to the federal Animal Welfare Act, the law governing animal care in laboratories and other nonfarm facilities. The amendments have yet to be implemented by the Department of Agriculture, which enforces the act (they remain stalled in the federal budget office). But they mark a new congressional commitment to the "three R's" preached by moderate groups like the Animal Welfare Institute and the Humane Society of the United States: *reduction* in the number of animals sacrificed, *refinement* of techniques that cause suffering and *replacement* of live animals with simulations or cell cultures.

Specifically, the amendments call for the creation of a national data bank that will list the results of all animal experiments and thus prevent needless repetition. All laboratories using live animals are required, under the amendments, to set up animal-care committees and submit to annual inspections. Facilities housing dogs must let them exercise, and those housing primates must provide for their "psychological well-being."

Rather than wait for the new rules to go into effect, many institutions have adopted reforms on their own. Most research facilities—including all that receive funds from the National Institutes of Health—now have committees that review proposed animal experiments. And some primate facilities, such as Yerkes and New York University's LEMSIP (Laboratory for Experimental Medicine and Surgery in Primates), are going out of their way to keep the animals mentally and emotionally stimulated. To encourage social contact among the 250 chimpanzees that LEMSIP uses in AIDS and hepatitis research, veterinarian James Mahoney has constructed wire-mesh tunnels between their cages. If an experiment requires keeping the animals separated, he makes sure they can see each other through sheets of Plexiglass. And to ward off the boredom that can turn lab chimps into blank-eyed psychotics, he gives them games.

Small Pleasures

He may place tubs of frozen Kool-Aid outside the chimps' cages, then give them pieces of plastic tubing that can be used as long-distance drinking straws. Noodling tube into tub for an occasional sip can provide hours of entertainment. In a variation on the theme, Mahoney passes out plastic tubes stuffed with raisins and marshmallows and lets the chimps use willow branches to extract the treats, just as they would termites from a hollow log in the wild. The animals' latest craze is cleaning their own teeth with toothbrushes and admiring the results in hand-held mirrors.

The reforms haven't been confined to research laboratories. For 50 years, consumer-protection laws have effectively required that cosmetics and household products be tested on animals before being sold to humans. But major firms have recently started seeking, and finding, less noxious methods of quality control. The LD-50 test, which consists of gauging the dose of a given substance needed to exterminate half of the animals in a test group, is already falling by the wayside; a survey by the Food and Drug Administration shows that its use has declined by 96 percent since the late 1970s. The Draize test for irritancy, which involves squirting high concentrations of possible irritants into the eyes of rabbits, is still the industry standard. But Procter & Gamble now exposes rabbits to concentrations somewhat closer to those a consumer might encounter. And it has joined other firms in pledging to halt all animal tests as soon as alternatives are available.

Still, the changes of the past decade hardly signal a new consensus on the proper use of animals. Some scientists consider the reforms excessive. University of Mississippi physiologist Arthur Guyton, for example, warns that the trend toward stricter regulation threatens the very future of science. Even the 1985 amendments to the Animal Welfare Act could prove ruinously expensive, he says. The "very arbitrary" rules governing cage size might force labs all over the country to renovate their facilities. "While medical research using animals has not been killed outright," Guyton concludes, "it is slowly bleeding to death."

Activists, for their part, complain that the reforms have been too modest. A lot of needless suffering is still being perpetrated in the name of science and medicine, they say. Consider the situation at Sema Inc., a government contract laboratory in Rockville, Md., where AIDS and hepatitis experiments are conducted on chimpanzees. Visitors aren't normally welcome, but the renowned primatologist Jane Goodall got a tour of the facility last year, and later wrote an article for The New York Times, describing what she saw.

Unlike LEMSIP's chimps, Sema's spend years of their lives in total isolation, confined to tiny boxes that resemble nothing so much as microwave ovens. After watching a chimp stare blankly into space as her caretaker approached, Goodall wrote, "I shall be haunted forever by her eyes and by the eyes of the other infant chimpanzees I saw that day. Have you ever looked into the eyes of a person who, stressed beyond endurance, has given up, succumbed utterly to the crippling helplessness of despair?" Katherine Bick, deputy director of the National Institutes of Health, denies that the situation is really so grim. She adds, as she did last spring, that larger, better cages are on the way. Meanwhile, says PETA's Pacheco, conditions sanctioned by the federal government are "needlessly driving intelligent animals insane."

Empty Cages

Even more divisive is the question of where science should be headed. Many activists dream of a day when all the cages are empty. "Our bottom line," says Newkirk, "is a day when there are no animals in labs." Researchers find that idea ludicrous. They tend to dismiss it as a product of ignorance ("People with no science education don't recognize that the pyramid of knowledge, built upon basic research, depends on animals," says one federal official), or of sentimentality ("a bizarre elevation of a touchy-feely, do-gooder's view of the world," in the words of Yerkes administrator Frederick King).

The moral dilemma behind all this bitterness was nicely crystallized in a recent report by the National Research Council. "Research with animals has saved human lives, lessened human suffering and advanced scientific understanding," the authors observe, "yet that same research can cause pain and distress for the animals involved and usually results in their death."

It would be nice, of course, if there were alternatives to vivisection that could deliver the same benefits without the death and suffering. But there is a limit to what can be accomplished with cell cultures and computer models. "You can't mathematically model this disease," says Murray Gardner, head of the U.C. Davis team studying early drug treatment in AIDS-infected monkeys. "You've got to experiment in a living system, where all the things we don't know about are going on."

The question is whether the practical benefits of vivisection constitute a moral justification for it. If mankind's interest in finding a better treatment for AIDS *doesn't* justify conducting lethal experiments on individual humans, an ethicist might ask, why does it justify performing them on monkeys? Why doesn't a monkey deserve moral consideration? What is the relevant difference between a human subject and an animal subject?

To reply that the human is *human* and the animal isn't only begs the question. Peter Singer likens it to sanctioning racial discrimination on the ground that white people are white and black people aren't. Another possible answer is that we humans enjoy certain *God-given* prerogatives. We are, after all, the only creatures the Bible says were made in God's image. "Most Judeo-Christian religions make distinctions about the special nature of man," says Frederick Goodwin, director of the Alcohol, Drug Abuse and Mental Health Administration. "To me, that is a distinct, qualitative difference between our primate relatives and man."

The Evidence?

It may be a difference, but it's not an empirical, observable one. It has to be taken on faith. Are there certain things *about* humans that make us inherently more valuable than other animals? Language and rational thought are the two traits usually cited as setting *Homo sapiens* apart. Yet there are plenty of humans who *lack* language and reason—babies, the senile, the insane—and the thought of performing medical experiments on them is abhorrent. Why, if a severely retarded child is too precious to sacrifice, is a chimp of superior intelligence fair game?

Maybe there is no reasoned moral justification. Maybe animal experimentation is best understood in purely practical terms, not as a prerogative or an obligation but as a strategy for survival. Whatever the answer, scientists can no longer afford to pretend that their critics' moral concerns are frivolous. Profound questions are being raised, and ignoring them won't make them go away.

ANIMAL RESEARCH IS UNNECESSARY AND DANGEROUS TO HUMAN HEALTH[2]

Can people love animals and still exploit them? Many people, including scientists like Nathaniel Comfort [who supports research using animals], have long tried to create a middle ground where they can use animals for "professional" reasons and yet claim to be an "animal lover" in private life. Comfort puts a New Age twist on his argument by citing a Native American tradition—showing a deep reverence for animals they must kill in order to eat—that he imitates by enjoying a live pet at home while continuing to work on his fellow fish at the lab. To this there is a simple reply: American Indians didn't kill to procure detailed

[2]Reprint of an article by Steve Siegal, animal rights activist. *Utne Reader.* 10:47-49. S/O '89. Copyright 1989 by Utne Reader. Reprinted by permission the author.

and esoteric knowledge that has no practical value. As for Comfort's contention that humans are just a little bit better than animals (and so it's justified to sparingly use them for "necessary" research), that's a totally unacceptable argument for those of us who oppose animal exploitation. His argument is simply another manifestation of a system that allows us to view other animals as our resources to do with as we wish. There is a basic immorality in forcing those weaker than us to be our testers.

Those who support animal research have always reduced the debate to a specter of human beings with horrible diseases whose only hope for a cure lies in animal research. And so it is that some 50 million animals are killed annually in U.S. labs for medical and scientific research. But today the truth of the matter is that animal research is unnecessary.

At the end of the last century when the anti-vivisection movement first flourished, researchers made convincing arguments that animal experimentation was indispensable to human health. Using a germ theory of infectious disease that called for creating animal models of each human disease, scientists isolated germs and inoculated them into lab animals, revealing the causative agents of major infectious diseases such as malaria, typhoid, and cholera. At this time opposition to vivisection was conducted primarily on ethical and humane grounds.

In the past two decades, all that has dramatically changed. As our main health problem, infectious diseases have been replaced by non-infectious, chronic degenerative diseases such as cancer, heart disease, stroke, and diabetes. Other medical problems such as AIDS, drug addiction, and schizophrenia are illnesses that develop in response to a complex set of factors caused by lifestyle, heredity, and environment. These modern health problems are the antithesis of the simple infectious diseases. Infectious diseases have a single irreducible cause—a germ that can be isolated and inoculated in animals whose bodies can hold the diseases like living test tubes, and thus can be experimented upon to test the efficiency of various drugs and treatments.

It's a tragedy and an outrage that the medical research establishment has held fast to the old animal model method of inquiry despite their inapplicability to the health problems we face today. The simple, undeniable truth is that animal research is done for the benefit of animal researchers. Billions of our tax dollars have been pocketed by "scientists" attempting to create animal models of every conceivable human problem from sexual impotence to manic depressive disorder to cancer. The almost $5 billion meted out annually in government grants is provided by taxpayers and represents guaranteed income for medical research firms independent of economic conditions or consumer demand.

The worst of this, of course, is the terrible price humans have been forced to pay as our most serious health afflictions have been allowed to flourish. Cancer death rates have increased each year for decades, and the 1985 death rate of 461,000 is almost four times the annual total of 50 years ago. The medical establishment's ineffectiveness against our number one killer—heart disease—has allowed the death toll to rise to 770,000 Americans each year. Diabetes, a rarity in the last century, is skyrocketing, along with a long list of other chronic degenerative diseases that will never be "solved" in a vivisector's laboratory.

Despite this and despite the fact that cancer and heart disease are known to be up to 80 percent preventable, these are the very areas in which the most tax dollars continue to be spent and the most animals continue to be killed. The result of this misdirection of resources is that the health of the American people is rapidly falling behind that of the rest of the western world. We are currently 20th in male life expectancy. We rank 23rd in infant mortality because of our failure to provide proper prenatal care. Facts like these make a dramatic case against the continued emphasis on creating diseases in animals at the expense of preventing them in humans.

It is impossible to mimic a chronic human disease in animals because of the biochemical, immunological, and physiological differences between the species. It is also impossible because researchers cannot understand the spontaneous process of disease by artificially placing it in the bodies of animals. We spend lavish sums of money on carcinogenicity studies in animals conducted to identify substances likely to cause cancer in humans. The two species used most often are mice and rats. A recent study found that 46 percent of the substances deemed carcinogenic in one of these two species were absolutely safe in the other.

Obviously, the same problems with using the animal model to predict causes of cancer in humans negate any ability to predict cures in humans. If drugs found effective on animals prove useful for human cancer patients it is merely coincidental; they are just as likely to prove useless or even to be harmful. The war on cancer has nothing other than a taxpayer-funded $11 billion gold rush for vivisectors. Animal experimentation has been a deplorable failure that hasn't produced a single substantial advance in the prevention or the treatment of human cancer. Indeed, of the ten most effective cancer drugs, not one was discovered through animal experimentation.

At best animal research is tacked on to legitimate advances inspired by clinical and epidemiological research. The only beneficiaries of this nonsense are the recipients of grants to "prove" in animals what had been previously demonstrated in people. At worst it has negative, sometimes devastating, effects on human health. Thalidomide, Oraflex, Flosint, Ibufenac, Chloramphenicol, Chlormycetin, Clioquinol, Isoproterenol, Phenformin, E Ferol, and Atromid S are but a few of the drugs that killed people after being found safe in exhaustive animal tests. Despite years of epidemiological and autopsy studies demonstrating that cigarette smoking causes lung cancer, health warnings were delayed and thousands died of cancer because of the difficulty in inducing smoking-caused cancer in lab animals.

These are the sound scientific arguments against animal research that have been vital to the animal protection movement's recent success . . . . It is evidence that the research establishment consistently ignores, focusing instead on inaccurate propaganda and specious ethical arguments to support their continued use of animals.

Despite my emphasis here on animal research's lack of scientific value, I believe more strongly than ever that animal research is a moral abomination that will come to be viewed as one of the foulest events in human history. The rationalizations of apologists like Comfort won't obscure the fact that people are not facing a choice between their own welfare and that of animals. The real choice before them is between the welfare of both people and animals against the vested financial interests of a small group that makes its living from animal exploitation.

ANIMAL RESEARCH IS CRITICAL
TO CONTINUED PROGRESS
IN HUMAN HEALTH[3]

In 1981, when she was seven years old, Gail Jaffe of Newton, Mass., was diagnosed as having Crohn's disease, an inflammatory bowel infection that wreaked havoc with her entire body, stunting her growth and causing malnutrition because she had difficulty digesting her food. For the next several years, the disease traumatized Gail and her family. Because she couldn't control her bowel movements, other children constantly teased and humiliated her.

Increasingly housebound, Gail's life became a depressing round of hospital visits, steroid injections, intravenous feedings, and operations, as doctors removed parts of her intestines in the effort to prevent the disease from spreading. "I remember my child looking at me and asking me if she was going to die," Gail's mother, Judy Jaffe, remembers. "I was able to look her in the eye and tell her truthfully that she would live because of medical techniques that came about from experiments on animals.

Today, Gail's disease is in remission—thanks, indeed, to medical advances made possible through animal research. All of the treatments used on Gail, ranging from the intravenous feedings to the operations, were developed after years of animal experimentation. Gail, of course, isn't the only person who has benefitted from animal research. Over the last century, biomedical researchers have developed surgical techniques, drugs, and treatments that have saved countless lives.

"We've witnessed an extraordinary outpouring of new drugs, devices and procedures to relieve human suffering and save lives," says Dr. Edward N. Brant, Jr., former Reagan Administration Assistant Secretary for Health and Human Services. "Very few of these advancements—maybe none of them—would have been possible without the use of vertebrate animals somewhere along the research path."

[3]Reprint of an article by Frankie L. Trull, president of the Foundation for Biomedical Research, New York. Reprinted from *USA Today*. Mr '88. pp 52+. Copyright 1988 by The Society for the Advancement of Education.

Knowledgeable people agree. Judy Rosner, executive director of the United Parkinson Foundation, says, "there is no way that further research can be done on Parkinson's disease without laboratory animals." Adds Dr. Leon Sternfeld, medical director of the United Cerebral Palsy Research and Educational Foundation, "Without animal research, the various types of preventive measures that we now have would not be possible."

Researchers use non-animal methodologies wherever possible. Nevertheless, they're grateful that they had animal research when they first began their investigations for cystic fibrosis. Dr. Sherry Keramidas, associate medical director of the Cystic Fibrosis Foundation, says that cystic fibrosis is an area where much of the current research is now done with cell cultures. She quickly notes, however, that "a lot of the early work was done with animals."

Medical Advances from Animal Research

To date some 41 Nobel Prizes have been awarded to scientists whose achievements depended, at least in part, on using laboratory animals. Vaccines against polio, diphtheria, mumps, measles, rubella, and smallpox would not have been possible without such experiments. Nor would there be such important techniques as open-heart surgery, brain surgery, coronary bypass, microsurgery to reattach limbs, organ transplants, and correction of congenital heart defects.

Insulin to control diabetes and medications important in the management of asthma, epilepsy, arthritis, ulcers, and hypertension are just a few medical advances that required animal research. The list goes on. It is safe to say that, if you are an American alive today, you most likely have benefited from animal research.

Animal research, for example, has played a vital role in the treatment of heart disease, the leading cause (nearly 40%) of deaths in the U.S. As a result of studies into causes, treatment, and prevention, the number of women killed by heart disease has declined by two percent a year since the early 1950's, while the number of men dying has been declining by the same rate since the late 1960's.

Nine-year-old Vanessa Carroll of Needham, Mass., is one of the many people who have benefited from heart research. At the age of 14 months, she was diagnosed as having a heart defect that required open-heart surgery. If she didn't have the operation, she would not live past the age of 10. "She was saved by the operation," says Vanessa's father, Michael Carroll, who is the financial director for the township of Needham.

Today, Vanessa is at the top of her class, but her father notes with pride that she is also the fastest runner in her class, even faster than the boys. "From some people's perspective a dog is as valuable as a human being," he says. "I guess you can't really argue with people like that, but I don't really understand it. I'll always believe that a human life like my daughter's is more important than an animal's."

His sentiments are echoed by Mrs. Linda Shelales of Bolton, Mass. Three years ago, her son, Matthew, was stricken by a virus that triggered an immune reaction in his body with inflamed and destroyed parts of his heart muscle. Experimental drugs that had been developed at Stanford University through laboratory animal experiments helped reduce the inflammation, but the damage to the heart was irreversible. The once robust 16-year-old began wasting away; his weight dropped by half, to just 92 pounds, and he hovered near death. The only solution, according to Matthew's doctors, was a heart transplant.

Heart transplants were first attempted with laboratory dogs at Stanford in the late 1950's. One of the problems researchers confronted was the body's rejection of the new heart. Since then, researchers around the nation have used dogs and other laboratory animals to develop drugs to prevent the body from rejecting a donated organ. All transplants remain difficult operations, but, because of the experience gained from using laboratory animals, such operations are increasingly successful. In fact, one reason why the Shelales decided to go ahead with Matthew's transplant was that the procedure had been tested many times on animals. "I would have never allowed even a drug near my son if it hadn't already been tested on animals," Mrs. Shelales says. Thus, in 1984, Matthew Shelales became only the second person in New England to undergo a heart transplant.

Today, Matthew is back up to 183 pounds and he was able to complete his high school education. He then worked in a pizzeria, in what his mother calls a high-stress job, while he took additional courses in preparation for college. In the fall of 1986, he entered Framingham State College, majoring in psychology.

Although the long-term prospects for heart transplant patients are unknown, Matthew has adjusted very well to his new heart, which gives his family hope. "We try not to worry," his mother says. "We have this feeling that he will be the first 70-year-old heart transplant patient."

As a result of what her son had undergone, Mrs. Shelales had her eyes opened to the value of biomedical experiments involving animals. She has come to feel so strongly about the beneficial nature of such experiments that she has testified before the Massachusetts legislature, when animal rights activists were trying to get legislators to curtail the use of research animals. "I'm a great animal lover, but I don't think some of these people have their priorities straight," she says. "If a ship is sinking and you have to decide to save your child or an animal, I'll save my child. There are many people like Matthew who are in a medical crisis."

Despite the efforts of biomedical researchers and laypeople like Mrs. Shelales to explain the importance of animal experiments, their voices are often drowned out by animal rightists. In recent years, these groups have launched well-financed legislative and publicity campaigns to end or severely restrict experiments on animals. In 1985, for instance, bills were introduced in 21 states that would have ended or restricted animal research; none was enacted.

Eight states, however, have already passed "pound laws," which ban or limit the use of pound animals in biomedical research, thereby driving up the cost of research—often to prohibitive levels. (Only about two percent of the more than 15,000,000 unwanted dogs and cats left in pounds and shelters each year are used in research; most of the rest are destroyed because new homes can not be found.)

In Massachusetts, for example, the pound law pushed the cost of dogs used in cardiovascular research to $325 apiece from $80 in 1984. The high price has forced some scientists using dogs in heart research to abandon that type of research, say researchers at Massachusetts General Hospital. It is estimated that 25% of heart research at Massachusetts General has been suspended as a result.

"We have a very serious situation," says Dr. John Powell, an associate professor at Harvard University and president of the Massachusetts Heart Association. "Heart disease is the number one killer in this country, and researchers trying to do something about the problem are having their hands tied [by animal rights activists]."

Misconceptions

Often, the animal rightists are, at best, misinformed. They claim that the number of animals used in scientific experimentation is increasing; figures offered range up to 100,000,000 animals used annually. In fact, the *only* recent study of biomedical research was issued by the U.S. Office of Technology Assessment and states that, by the best current estimates, the number of animals used is between 17 and 22,000,000. That number actually represents a decline from 38,000,000 in 1968, according to a study by the National Academy of Sciences.

In addition, animal rights activists repeatedly imply that experiments are preformed on pets. "Thefts of dogs and cats are on the increase," a representative of the Humane Society of the U.S. recently warned. "Until we stop the use of pet-type animals in laboratory research, we won't be able to stop the theft of pet animals." Such appeals, which serve to frighten pet owners, rarely have basis in fact. In a Foundation for Biomedical Research survey of police departments and animal control agencies in the nation's 10 largest cities, there have been no reports of such thefts for resale to research or education.

Indeed, approximately 90%—the overwhelming majority of animals used in research—are rats, mice, and other rodents. Less than one percent are dogs and cats, but they are an important one percent. Dogs are essential to study of the cardiovascular system and to the development of ways to treat and prevent diseases of the heart and arteries. Cats are vital to certain studies of vision and hearing, as well as brain function.

Another misconception purports that other research methods can replace the use of animals in biomedical research. Unfortunately, there are no real alternatives to animal research. In the course of biomedical investigation, science has developed many valuable non-animal research models, such as tissue and cell cultures and computer models, which are useful in a few types of research and often can supplement work with live animals. In the immediate future, they are most promising in the field of toxicology testing. They are to be encouraged where scientifically valid. However, chemical compounds and medical procedures must also be tested on living systems—made up of interrelated organs and organ systems—before they can be tried in human beings. It is unrealistic to believe that all animal research can be done away with today—or in the forseeable future—in favor of such adjunct methodologies. To do so, or to shift funds from ongoing investigations into those using only adjunct technologies—the agenda of many animal rights groups—would doom generations of human patients to a future without hope.

The truth is that animal research is essential. There are strong economic pressures against the unnecessary use of laboratory animals or any other research resources. There are only limited funds available for study of the wide range of human health problems that require research. Funding agencies, therefore, must restrict support to those studies that will lead to new knowledge of the body and greater understanding of the cause, cure, and prevention of diseases. For example, the National Institutes of Health, the nation's largest single source of support for biomedical research, is able to fund only about one-third of all research proposals that have been judged scientifically worthy. This process serves to weed out waste of any research resources; it minimizes the possibility that laboratory animals will be used for trivial purposes.

In addition, laws and regulations protect laboratory animals. There are Federal standards set forth in the Animal Welfare Act for the care and treatment of laboratory animals, including housing, feeding, cleanliness, ventilation, and veterinary care. The law also contains provisions for the use of anesthesia or pain-killing drugs for potentially painful procedures and for post-operative care. In addition, the U.S. Public Health Service requires adherence to its Animal Welfare Policy by all institutions receiving research grants from the National Institutes of Health. Under the terms of the Animal Welfare Policy, institutions must follow the detailed recommendations on animal care and treatment that are contained in a book called the *Guide for the Care and Use of Laboratory Animals*. The policy also mandates review of all research by an animal care and use committee set up in each institution, to make certain that laboratory animals are being used responsibly and treated humanely.

One of the most important protections for laboratory animals, however, does not appear in any law or guideline. The fact is, good care contributes to good science—the goal of every researcher. Scientists need the best possible conditions for their animals in order to insure the best possible scientific results of their investigations. Mistreatment of research animals will reduce the reliability of the results of the study, something the researcher must prevent. The Foundation for Biomedical Research supports only the highest standards of laboratory care for both humane and scientific reasons. In fact, many animal welfare organizations have joined with scientific organizations such as the National Association for Biomedical Research in order to secure increased funding for laboratory inspections by the U.S. Department of Agriculture, which is charged with enforcing the Animal Welfare Act.

Another fallacy promoted by animal rights advocates is that all laboratory animals suffer great pain and distress. Most biomedical research does not result in pain or significant distress to the animals. A survey of research facilities released in 1985 by the Department of Agriculture showed that the majority of experiments using animal subjects (62%) involve no pain for the animal. In another 32% of the studies, the animals feel no pain because they receive either anesthesia or pain-killing drugs. In a few experiments (six percent), anesthesia and analgesics must be withheld because they would obscure the results of the research. An example of such a study would be one on pain, itself a major human health problem.

Attacking and distorting complex scientific procedures that use animals, however, is nothing new. In the 19th century, for example, animal rights activists attacked Edward Jenner's vaccine for smallpox and Louis Pasteur's germ theory of infection because the scientists used animals in their investigations. In Jenner's case, antivivisectionists contended that vaccination not only harmed animals, but hurt humans and would "result in a degenerate race."

The more radical of today's animal rightists take their cause to levels their forebears never considered. "How then can one species, ours, consider it has the right to deny others their basic interests in liberty and life?," one group's representative asks.

Perhaps the question can best be answered only by someone such as Irene Whittemore of Pembroke, Mass., who was diagnosed as having leukemia in 1983. Her physician told her that, just 15 years ago, she wouldn't have had a chance to live. Yet, because of chemotherapies that were developed on animals, her leukemia is in remission.

Today, she is alive and married, with a young daughter. Now, she hopes that scientists will continue to pursue advances that will make it easier and less painful to treat cancer. Although her leukemia is in remission, she also hopes that further advances will be made so that she can be treated once again if her disease becomes active. "I would certainly not be here if it wasn't for laboratory animals," she says. "I guess that's selfish, but I also have a daughter and a husband now. They would find it hard to live without me."

HUMAN VS ANIMAL RIGHTS[4]

For centuries, opposition has been directed against the use of animals for the benefit of humans. For more than four centuries in Europe, and for more than a century in the United States, this opposition has targeted scientific research that involves animals. More recent movements in support of animal rights have arisen in an attempt to impede, if not prohibit, the use of animals in scientific experimentation. These movements employ various means that range from information and media campaigns to destruction of property and threats against investigators. The latter efforts have resulted in the identification of more militant animal rights bands as terrorist groups. The American Medical Association has long been a defender of humane research that employs animals, and it is very concerned about the efforts of animal rights and welfare groups to interfere with research. Recently, the Association prepared a detailed analysis of the controversy over the use of animals in research, and the consequences for research and clinical medicine if the philosophy of animal rights activists were to prevail in society. This article is a condensation of the Association's analysis.

Research with animals is a highly controversial topic in our society. Animal rights groups that intend to stop all experimentation with animals are in the vanguard of this controversy. Their methods range from educational efforts directed in large measure to the young and uninformed, to promotion of restrictive legislation, filing lawsuits, and violence that includes raids on laboratories and death threats to investigators. Their rhetoric is emotionally charged and their information is frequently distorted

[4]Reprint of an AMA position paper by Jerod M. Loeb, Ph.D., William R. Hendee, Ph.D., Steven J. Smith, Ph.D., and M. Roy Schwarz, M.D. *The Journal of the American Medical Association.* 262:2716-20. N 17, '89. Copyright 1989 by the American Medical Association.

and pejorative. Their tactics vary but have a single objective—to stop scientific research with animals.

The resources of the animal rights groups are extensive, in part because less militant organizations of animal activists, including some humane societies, have been infiltrated or taken over by animal rights groups to gain access to their fiscal and physical holdings. Through bizarre tactics, extravagant claims, and gruesome myths, animal rights groups have captured the attention of the media and a sizable segment of the public. Nevertheless, people invariably support the use of animals in research when they understand both sides of the issue and the contributions of animal research to relief of human suffering. However, all too often they do not understand both sides because information about the need for animal research is not presented. When this need is explained, the presentation often reveals an arrogance of the scientific community and an unwillingness to be accountable to public opinion.

The use of animals in research is fundamentally an ethical question: is it more ethical to ban all research with animals or to use a limited number of animals in research under humane conditions when no alternatives exist to achieve medical advances that reduce substantial human suffering and misery? This question has been addressed at length in a White Paper on Animal Research prepared by the American Medical Association. This article is a condensation of the White Paper; the complete paper can be obtained from the Office of the Vice President for Science and Technology, American Medical Association, 535 N Dearborn St, Chicago, IL 60610.

Animals in Scientific Research

Animals have been used in research for more than 2000 years. In the third century BC, the natural philosopher Erisistratus of Alexandria used animals to study bodily function. In all likelihood, Aristotle performed vivisection on animals. The Roman physician Galen used apes and pigs to prove his theory that veins carry blood rather than air. In succeeding centuries, animals were employed to confirm theories about physiology developed through observation. Advances in knowledge from these experiments include demonstration of the circulation of blood by Harvey in 1622, documentation of the effects of anesthesia on the body in 1846, and elucidation of the relationship between bacteria and disease in 1878. In his book *An Introduction to the Study of Experimental Medicine* published in 1865, Bernard described the importance of animal research to advances in knowledge about the human body and justified the continued use of animals for this purpose.

In this century, many medical advances have been achieved through research with animals. Infectious diseases such as pertussis, rubella, measles, and poliomyelitis have been brought under control with vaccines developed in animals. The development of immunization techniques against today's infectious diseases, including human immunodeficiency virus disease [HIV], depends entirely on experiments in animals. Antibiotics that control infection are always tested in animals before use in humans. Physiological disorders such as diabetes and epilepsy are treatable today through knowledge and products gained by animal research. Surgical procedures such as coronary artery bypass grafts, cerebrospinal fluid shunts, and retinal reattachments have evolved from experiments with animals. Transplantation procedures for persons with failed liver, heart, lung, and kidney function are products of animal research.

Animals have been essential to the evolution of modern medicine and the conquest of many illnesses. However, many medical challenges remain to be solved. Cancer, heart disease, cerebrovascular disease, dementia, depression, arthritis, and a variety of inherited disorders are yet to be understood and controlled. Until they are, human pain and suffering will endure, and society will continue to expend its emotional and fiscal resources in efforts to alleviate or at least reduce them.

Animal research has not only benefited humans. Procedures and products developed through this process have also helped animals. Vaccines against rabies, distemper, and parvovirus in dogs are a spin-off of animal research, as are immunization techniques against cholera in hogs, encephalitis in horses, and brucellosis in cattle. Drugs to combat heartworm, intestinal parasites, and mastitis were developed in animals used for experimental purposes. Surgical procedures developed in animals help animals as well as humans.

Research with animals has yielded immeasurable benefits to both humans and animals. However, this research raises fundamental philosophical issues concerning the rights of humans to use animals to benefit humans and other animals. If these rights are granted (and many people are loath to do so), additional

questions arise concerning the way that research should be performed, the accountability of researchers to public sentiment, the
nature of an ethical code for animal research, and who should
compose and approve the code. Today, some animal activists are
asking whether humans have the right to exercise dominion over
animals for any purpose, including research. Others suggest that
because humans have dominion over other forms of life, they are
obligated to protect and preserve animals and ensure that they
are not exploited. Still others agree that animals can be used to
help people, but only under circumstances that are so structured
as to be unattainable by most researchers. These attitudes may all
differ, but their consequences are similar. They all threaten to
diminish or stop animal research.

Challenge to Animal Research

Challenges to the use of animals to benefit humans are not
new—their origins can be traced back several centuries. With
respect to animal research, opposition has been vocal in Europe
for more than 400 years and in the United States for at least 100
years.

Most of the current arguments against research with animals
have historic precedents that must be grasped to understand the
current debate. These precedents originated in the controversy
between Cartesian and utilitarian philosophers that extended
from the 16th to the 18th centuries.

The Cartesian-utilitarian debate was opened by the French
philosopher Descartes, who defended the use of animals in experiments by insisting the animals respond to stimuli in only one
way—"according to the arrangement of their organs." He stated
that animals lack the ability to reason and think and are, therefore, similar to a machine. Humans, on the other hand, can think,
talk, and respond to stimuli in various ways. These differences,
Descartes argued, make animals inferior to humans and justify
their use as a machine, including as experimental subjects. He
proposed that animals learn only by experience, whereas humans
learn by "teaching-learning." Humans do not always have to experience something to know that it is true.

Descartes' arguments were countered by the utilitarian philosopher Bentham of England. "The question," said Bentham, "is
not can they reason? nor, can they talk? but can they suffer?" In
utilitarian terms, humans and animals are linked by their com-

mon ability to suffer and their common right not to suffer and die at the hands of others. This utilitarian thesis has rippled through various groups opposed to research with animals for more than a century.

In the 1970s, the antivivisectionist movement was influenced by three books that clarified the issues and introduced the rationale for increased militancy against animal research. In 1971, the anthology *Animals, Men and Morals,* by Godlovitch et al, raised the concept of animal rights and analyzed the relationships between humans and animals. Four years later, *Victims of Science,* by Ryder, introduced the concept of "speciesism" as equivalent to fascism. Also in 1975, Singer published *Animal Liberation: A New Ethic for Our Treatment of Animals.* This book is generally considered the progenitor of the modern animal rights movement. Invoking Ryder's concept of speciesism, Singer deplored the historic attitude of humans toward nonhumans as a "form of prejudice no less objectionable than racism or sexism." He urged that the liberation of animals should become the next great cause after civil rights and the women's movement.

Singer's book not only was a philosophical treatise; it also was a call to action. It provided an intellectual foundation and a moral focus for the animal rights movement. These features attracted many who were indifferent to the emotional appeal based on a love of animals that had characterized antivivisectionist efforts for the past century. Singer's book swelled the ranks of the antivivisectionist movement and transformed it into a movement for animal rights. It also has been used to justify illegal activities intended to impede animal research and instill fear and intimidation in those engaged in it.

Animal Rights Activism

The animal rights movement is supported financially by a wide spectrum of individuals, most of whom are well-meaning persons who care about animals and wish to see them treated humanely. Many of these supporters do not appreciate the diverse philosophies and activities of different groups of animal activists, and they have not explored differences between animal welfare and animal rights in any depth. They believe that their financial contributions pay for animal shelters and efforts to find homes for stray animals. They do not realize that their contributions also support illegal activities that have been classified as terrorist actions by the U.S. Federal Bureau of Investigation and the New Scotland Yard. Many of these illegal activities are conducted by a clandestine group called the Animal Liberation Front. Other groups alledged to be engaged in illegal activities include Earth First, Last Chance for Animals, People for the Ethical Treatment of Animals, Band of Mercy, and True Friends.

In the United States, illegal activities conducted by these groups since July 1988 include the following (F. Trull, personal communication):

- break-in, theft, and arson at the University of Arizona in Tucson, with more than 1000 animals stolen and arson damage of $250,000;
- break-in and theft at Duke University in Durham, NC;
- break-in and theft at the Veterans Administration Medical Center in Tucson (Arizona);
- bomb threat to the director of the lab animal facility, Stanford (Calif.) University;
- attempted bombing, U.S. Surgical Corporation, Norwalk, Conn;
- vandalism, University of California, Santa Cruz; and
- break-in and theft, Loma Linda (Calif.) University.

Illegal actions have been pursued with even greater vigor in the United Kingdom.

Recent examples related to medical research in the United Kingdom include the following (M. Macleod, personal communication):

- home and car damage of two investigators at a Wellcome research facility;
- home and car damage of three investigators at St. George's Hospital, Tooting;
- bomb planted and warning given to director of construction firm building laboratory for Glaxo Corporation;
- five incendiary devices that caused $50,000 damage to company that supplied portable offices to Glaxo Corporation during laboratory construction;
- property damage at Bromley High School, where animals are used in dissection classes; and
- mailing of hundreds of incendiary devices, including one to Prime Minister Margaret Thatcher.

Other countries that experienced similar terrorist activities include Italy, Japan, New Zealand, Sweden, Holland, Belgium, Canada, and West Germany. Some officials believe that these activities are part of an international conspiracy operating under the rubric of animal rights but dedicated to general anarchy. They also feel that support for these efforts is derived principally from thousands of well-meaning but naive individuals who contribute to organizations that plead the cause of animal welfare but actually serve as fronts for terrorist activities.

Defense of Animal Research

The issue of animal research is fundamentally an issue of the dominion of humans over animals. This issue is rooted in the Judeo-Christian religion of western culture, including the ancient tradition of animal sacrifice described in the Old Testament and the practice of using animals as surrogates for suffering humans described in the New Testament. The sacredness of human life is a central theme of biblical morality, and the dominion of humans over other forms of life is a natural consequence of this theme. The issue of dominion is not, however, unique to animal research. It is applicable to every situation where animals are subservient to humans. It applies to the use of animals for food and clothing; the application of animals as beasts of burden and transportation; the holding of animals in captivity such as in zoos and as household pets; the use of animals as entertainment, such as in sea parks and circuses; the exploitation of animals in sports that employ animals, including hunting, racing, and animal shows; and the eradication of pests such as rats and mice from homes and farms. Even provision of food and shelter to animals reflects an attitude of dominion of humans over animals. A person who truly does not believe in human dominance over animals would be forced to oppose all of these practices, including keeping animals as household pets or in any form of physical or psychological captivity. Such a posture would defy tradition evolved over the entire course of human existence.

Some animal advocates do not take issue with the right of humans to exercise dominion over animals. They agree that animals are inferior to humans because they do not possess attributes such as a moral sense and concepts of past and future. However, they also claim that it is precisely because of these differences that humans are obligated to protect animals and not exploit them for the selfish betterment of humans. In their view, animals are like infants and the mentally incompetent, who must be nurtured and protected from exploitation. This view shifts the issues of domin-

ion from one of rights claimed by animals to one of responsibilities exercised by humans.

Neither of these philosophical positions addresses the issue of
animal research from the perspective of the immorality of not
using animals in research. From this perspective, depriving humans (and animals) of advances in medicine that result from
research with animals is inhumane and fundamentally unethical.
Spokespersons for this perspective suggest that patients with dementia, stroke, disabling injuries, heart disease, and cancer deserve relief from suffering, and that depriving them of hope and
relief by eliminating animal research is an immoral and uncon-
scionable act. Defenders of animal research claim that animals
sometimes must be sacrificed in the development of methods to
relieve pain and suffering of humans (and animals) and to affect
treatments and cures of a variety of human maladies.

The immeasurable benefits of animal research to humans are
undeniable. One example is the development of a vaccine for
poliomyelitis, with the result that the number of cases of poliomyelitis in the United States alone declined from 58,000 in 1952 to 4
in 1984. Benefits of this vaccine worldwide are even more
impressive.

Every year, hundreds of thousands of humans are spared the
braces, wheelchairs, and iron lungs required for the victims of
poliomyelitis who survive this infectious disease. The research
that led to a poliomyelitis vaccine required the sacrifice of hundreds of primates. Without this sacrifice, development of the vaccine would have been impossible, and in all likelihood the poliomyelitis epidemic would have continued unabated. Depriving
humanity of this medical advance is unthinkable to almost all
persons. Other diseases that are curable or treatable today as a
result of animal research include diphtheria, scarlet fever, tuber-
culosis, diabetes, and appendicitis. Human suffering would be
much more stark today if these diseases, and many others as well,
had not been amendable to treatment and cure through advances
obtained by animal research.

Issues in Animal Research

Animal rights groups have several stock arguments against
animal research. Some of these issues are described and refuted
herein.

THE CLINICAL VALUE OF BASIC RESEARCH

Persons opposed to research with animals often claim that basic biomedical research has no clinical value and therefore does not justify the use of animals. However, basic research is the foundation for most medical advances and consequently for progress in clinical medicine. Without basic research, including that with animals, chemotherapeutic advances against cancer (including childhood leukemia and breast malignancy), beta-blockers for cardiac patients, and electrolyte infusions for patients with dysfunctional metabolism would never have been achieved.

DUPLICATION OF EXPERIMENTS

Opponents of animal research frequently claim that experiments are needlessly duplicated. However, the duplication of results is an essential part of the confirmation process in science. The generalization of results from one laboratory to another prevents anomalous results in one laboratory from being interpreted as scientific truth. The cost of research animals, the need to publish the results of experiments, and the desire to conduct meaningful research all function to reduce the likelihood of unnecessary experiments. Furthermore, the intense competition for research funds and the peer review process lessen the probability of obtaining funds for unnecessary research. Most scientists are unlikely to waste valuable time and resources conducting unnecessary experiments when opportunities for performing important research are so plentiful.

THE NUMBER OF ANIMALS USED IN RESEARCH

Animal rights groups claim that as many as 150 million animals are used in research each year, most of them needlessly. However, the U.S. Office of Technology Assessment has estimated that only 17 to 22 million animals were involved in experimental studies in 1983, including 12.2 to 15.2 million rats and mice bred especially for research. Also used were 2.5 to 4 million fish, 100,000 to 500,000 amphibians, 100,000 to 500,000 birds, 500,000 to 550,000 rabbits, 500,000 guinea pigs, 450,000 hamsters, 182,000 to 195,000 dogs, 55,000 to 60,000 cats, and 54,000 to 59,000 primates.

Animal activists claim that research with animals is institutionalized and that investigators do not consider ways to reduce the number of animals involved in research. In contrast, evidence suggests that the number of research animals is decreasing each year, according to surveys by the National Research Council of the National Academy of Sciences. In 1978, for example, the Council estimated that the total of 20 million research animals was 50% less than the number for 1968.

The number of animals used in research is limited by the cost of animals (especially in the present period of limited funds for research), the availability and expense of facilities to house them, and by the compassion of investigators to use no more animals than needed to perform meaningful research. It also is controlled by institutional animal-use committees that are empowered to monitor animal experimentation to ensure that experimental design is appropriate and animals are treated humanely and compassionately. These committees also are obligated to ensure that animals are properly housed and cared for. The performance of these committees is evaluated by various federal and voluntary agencies, including the American Association of Laboratory Animal Care.

THE USE OF PRIMATES IN RESEARCH

Animal activists often make a special plea on behalf of non-human primates, and many of the sit-ins, demonstrations, and break-ins have been directed at primate research centers. Efforts to justify these activities invoke the premise that primates are much like humans because they exhibit suffering and other emotions.

Keeping primates in cages and isolating them from others of their kind is considered by activists as cruel and destructive of their "psychological well-being." However, the opinion that animals that resemble humans most closely and deserve the most protection and care reflects an attitude of speciesism (ie, a hierarchical scheme of relative importance) that most activists purportedly abhor. This logical fallacy in the drive for special protection of primates apparently escapes most of its adherents.

Some scientific experiments require primates exactly because they simulate human physiology so closely. Primates are susceptible to many of the same diseases as humans and have similar immune systems. They also possess intellectual, cognitive, and social skills above those of other animals. These characteristics make primates invaluable in research related to language, perception, and visual and spatial skills. Although primates constitute only 0.5% of all animals used in research, their contributions have been essential to the continued acquisition of knowledge in the biological and behavioral sciences.

Do Animals Suffer Needless Pain and Abuse?

Animal activists frequently assert that research with animals causes severe pain and that many research animals are abused either deliberately or through indifference. Actually, experiments today involve pain only when relief from pain would interfere with the purpose of the experiments. In any experiment in which an animal might experience pain, federal law requires that a veterinarian must be consulted in planning the experiment, and anesthesia, tranquilizers, and analgesics must be used except when they would compromise the results of the experiment.

In 1984, the Department of Agriculture reported that 61% of research animals were not subjected to painful procedures, and another 31% received anesthesia or pain-relieving drugs. The remaining 8% did experience pain, often because improved understanding and treatment of pain, including chronic pain, were the purpose of the experiment. Chronic pain is a challenging health problem that costs the United States about $50 billion a year in direct medical expenses, lost productivity, and income.

Alternatives to the Use of Animals

One of the most frequent objections to animal research is the claim that alternative research models obviate the need for research with animals. The concept of alternatives was first raised in 1959 by Russell and Burch in their book, *The Principles of Humane Experimental Technique*. These authors exhorted scientists to reduce the pain of experimental animals, decrease the number of animals used in research, and replace animals with nonanimal models whenever possible.

However, more often than not, alternatives to research animals are not available. In certain research investigations, cell, tissue, and organ cultures and computer models can be used as adjuncts to experiments with animals, and occasionally as substitutes for animals, at least in preliminary phases of the investigations. However, in many experimental situations, culture techniques and computer models are wholly inadequate because they do not encompass the physiological complexity of the whole animal. Examples where animals are essential to research include development of a vaccine against human immunodeficiency virus [HIV], refinement of organ transplantation techniques, investigation of mechanical devices as replacements for and adjuncts to physiological organs, identification of target-specific pharmaceuticals for cancer diagnosis and treatment, restoration of infarcted myocardium in patients with cardiac disease, evolution of new diagnostic imaging technologies, improvement of methods to relieve mental stress and anxiety, and evaluation of approaches to define and treat chronic pain. These challenges can only be addressed by research with animals as an essential step in the evolution of knowledge that leads to solutions. Humans are the only alternatives to animals for this step. When faced with this alternative, most people prefer the use of animals as the research model.

Comment

Love of animals and concern for their welfare are admirable characteristics that distinguish humans from other species of animals. Most humans, scientists as well as laypersons, share these attributes. However, when the concern for animals impedes the development of methods to improve the welfare of humans through amelioration and elimination of pain and suffering, a fundamental choice must be made. This choice is present today in the conflict between animal rights activism and scientific research. The American Medical Association made this choice more than a century ago and continues to stand squarely in defense of the use of animals for scientific research. In this position, the Association is supported by opinion polls that reveal strong endorsement of the American public for the use of animals in research and testing.

The philosophical position of animal rights activists would require a total ban on research with animals. The consequences of such a ban were described in a 1986 report to Congress by the U.S. Office of Technology Assessment: "Implementation of this option would effectively arrest most basic biomedical and behavioral research and toxicological testing in the United States." The economic and public health consequences of that option, the U.S.

Office of Technology Assessment warned, "are so unpredictable and speculative" that this course of action should be considered dangerous. Although laws to ban the use of animals in research have been introduced into a number of states' legislatures, neither a majority of the American people nor their elected representatives have supported them.

Terrorist acts are a serious threat to biomedical research and to the safety and security of those involved in it. However, such desperate acts are unlikely to stop the use of animals in research. The greater threat to research is legislation that imposes restrictions on how animals are housed and cared for that cost more than the research community can afford. Existing federal and state laws, together with peer review and supervision by institutions and funding agencies, provide adequate protection against misuse and abuse of animals. Additional legislation does not offer increased protection. It only increases the expense of research and, in some cases, stops it entirely by imposing exorbitant costs and demands.

The American Medical Association believes that research involving animals is absolutely essential to maintaining and improving the health of people in America and worldwide. Animal research is required to develop solutions to human tragedies such as human immunodeficiency virus disease, cancer, heart disease, dementia, stroke, and congenital and developmental abnormalities. The American Medical Association recognizes the moral obligation of investigators to use alternatives to animals whenever possible, and to conduct their research with animals as humanely as possible. However, it is convinced that depriving humans of medical advances by preventing research with animals is philosophically and morally a fundamentally indefensible position. Consequently, the American Medical Association is committed to the preservation of animal research and to the conduct of this research under the most humane conditions possible.

A SCIENTIST: "I AM THE ENEMY"[5]

I am the enemy! One of those vilified, inhumane physician-scientists involved in animal research. How strange, for I have never thought of myself as an evil person. I became a pediatrician because of my love for children and my desire to keep them healthy. During medical school and residency, however, I saw many children die of leukemia, prematurity and traumatic injury—circumstances against which medicine has made tremendous progress, but still has far to go. More important, I also saw children, alive and healthy, thanks to advances in medical science such as infant respirators, potent antibiotics, new surgical techniques and the entire field of organ transplantation. My desire to tip the scales in favor of the healthy, happy children drew me to medical research.

My accusers claim that I inflict torture on animals for the sole purpose of career advancement. My experiments supposedly have no relevance to medicine and are easily replaced by computer simulation. Meanwhile, an apathetic public barely watches, convinced that the issue has no significance, and publicity-conscious politicians increasingly give way to the demands of the activists.

We in medical research have also been unconsciously apathetic. We have allowed the most extreme animal-rights protesters to seize the initiative and frame the issue as one of "animal fraud." We have been complacent in our belief that a knowledgeable public would sense the importance of animal research to the public health. Perhaps we have been mistaken in not responding to the emotional tone of the argument created by those sad posters of animals by waving equally sad posters of children dying of leukemia or cystic fibrosis.

Much is made of the pain inflicted on these animals in the name of medical science. The animal-rights activists contend that this is evidence of our malevolent and sadistic nature. A more reasonable argument, however, can be advanced in our defense. Life is often cruel, both to animals and human beings. Teenagers get thrown from the back of a pickup truck and suffer severe

[5]Reprint of a guest editorial by Ron Karpati, pediatrician and immunological researcher. *Newsweek.* 114:12-3. D 18 '89. Copyright 1989 by Newsweek.

head injuries. Toddlers, barely able to walk, find themselves at the bottom of a swimming pool while a parent checks the mail. Physicians hoping to alleviate the pain and suffering these tragedies cause have but three choices: create an animal model of the injury or disease and use that model to understand the process and test new therapies; experiment on human beings—some experiments will succeed, most will fail—or finally, leave medical knowledge static, hoping that accidental discoveries will lead us to the advances.

Some animal-rights activists would suggest a fourth choice, claiming that computer models can simulate animal experiments, thus making the actual experiments unnecessary. Computers can simulate, reasonably well, the effects of well-understood principles on complex systems, as in the application of the laws of physics to airplane and automobile design. However, when the principles themselves are in question, as is the case with the complex biological systems under study, computer modeling alone is of little value.

One of the terrifying effects of the effort to restrict the use of animals in medical research is that the impact will not be felt for years and decades: drugs that might have been discovered will not be; surgical techniques that might have been developed will not be, and fundamental biological processes that might have been understood will remain mysteries. There is the danger that politically expedient solutions will be found to placate a vocal minority, while the consequences of those decisions will not be apparent until long after the decisions are made and the decision makers forgotten.

Fortunately, most of us enjoy good health, and the trauma of watching one's child die has become a rare experience. Yet our good fortune should not make us unappreciative of the health we enjoy or the advances that make it possible. Vaccines, antibiotics, insulin and drugs to treat heart disease, hypertension and stroke are all based on animal research. Most complex surgical procedures, such as coronary-artery bypass and organ transplantation, are initially developed in animals. Presently undergoing animal studies are techniques to insert genes in humans in order to replace the defective ones found to be the cause of so much disease. These studies will effectively end if animal research is severely restricted.

In America today, death has become an event isolated from our daily existence—out of the sight and thoughts of most of us.

As a doctor who has watched many children die, and their parents grieve, I am particularly angered by people capable of so much compassion for a dog or a cat, but with seemingly so little for a dying human being. These people seem so insulated from the reality of human life and death and what it means.

Make no mistake, however: I am not advocating the needlessly cruel treatment of animals. To the extent that the animal-rights movement has made us more aware of the needs of these animals, and made us search harder for suitable alternatives, they have made a significant contribution. But if the more radical members of this movement are successful in limiting further research, their efforts will bring about a tragedy that will cost many lives. The real question is whether an apathetic majority can be aroused to protect its future against a vocal, but misdirected, minority.

ALTERNATIVES TO ANIMALS IN TOXICITY TESTING[6]

Each year thousands of chemicals undergo rigorous testing designed to evaluate their potential toxicity. Almost all of the tests take place in animals: the reactions of rats, rabbits and mice to chemicals are currently the best available predictors of the effects the substances will have on the human organism. The introduction of animal testing in the U.S. in the 1920's was a major advance in toxicity testing, and subsequent debates about the place of animals in testing were qualified by the absence of better alternatives.

In the past decade the issue of whole-animal toxicity testing has become more urgent and contentious. Animal-welfare advocates have decried the suffering of millions of animals, and industries bringing chemicals to the marketplace have begun to chafe at the costs and delays imposed by animal testing. Meanwhile, case histories such as that of thalidomide serve to remind the

[6]Reprint of an article by Alan M. Goldberg, director of the Center for Alternatives to Animal Testing, Johns Hopkins University, and John M. Frazier, director of the center's In Vitro Toxicology Laboratory. *Scientific American.* 261:24+. Ag '89. Reprinted with permission. Copyright 1989 by Scientific American, Inc. All rights reserved.

public and testing establishments alike of the perils of letting unsafe chemicals reach the marketplace. In answer to these concerns, toxicologists began exploring possible alternatives.

Their exploration has yielded a new methodology known as in vitro toxicity testing. Literally, *in vitro* means "in glass," but biologists interpret the term more broadly to mean research that does not involve intact higher animals. In vitro testing includes a battery of living systems—bacteria, cultured animal cells, fertilized chicken eggs, frog embryos—that can be employed to evaluate the toxicity of chemicals in human beings. Ultimately workers hope to be able to test chemicals in cultures of human cells from various organs and tissues so that the question of human toxicity can be answered more directly.

Several factors have paved the way for the introduction of in vitro testing. One is the growth of the science of toxicology itself. Today investigators understand much better how toxicological processes are begun and how toxic effects are expressed; they need not use the death or illness of an animal as an end point in their studies. Another factor has to do with technological developments of the past few years. New options in culture techniques and bioanalytical tools allow workers to monitor toxicity with unprecedented thoroughness and precision at the cellular level rather than at the organismal level.

Yet the obstacles such efforts face are tremendous. Some are technical: singly or in combination, in vitro tests as yet cannot approximate the complexity of interactions that take place in a living animal. Some of the obstacles are bureaucratic: no framework has been established for approving in vitro test procedures or for incorporating the results of such tests into the evaluation of results from whole-animal, or in vivo, methods.

We believe in vitro tests will eventually be able to meet these challenges. Protocols for in vitro tests already exist that can complement the current panoply of whole-animal procedures and reduce the number of animals that are subjected to testing. It is not too soon to begin planning ways to integrate in vitro testing into toxicity testing as a whole.

Toxicity testing is one of the two major components of risk assessment, the process by which new substances are evaluated for their potential impact on human health and welfare. The other component is assessment of exposure. The exposure estimate indicates how many people will be exposed to a chemical in what concentrations, for how long and under what conditions. For a chemical to pose a risk of notable proportion, there must exist the likelihood of human exposure to the agent in quantities sufficient to produce adverse biological effects.

Toxicity testing is required for new chemicals introduced into the marketplace, old chemicals that are proposed for new uses and new mixtures of old or new chemicals. The main objectives of such testing are twofold. The first objective, known as hazard identification, involves determining which potential adverse effects—cancer, kidney damage, reproductive injury and so on—can ensue from exposure to a given chemical. The second objective is to provide data estimating the quantitative exposure-response relationship for the chemical in human beings and other organisms.

The exposure-response relationship describes the likelihood of an organisms' developing a particular adverse biological response as a function of its exposure to the chemical. Such a relationship presumably exists for each of the hazards identified for a given chemical. It may vary, however, depending on how a person is exposed to the chemical—whether through ingestion, inhalation or contact with the skin. The age, genetic makeup and nutritional status of the person may play a role as well.

The LD50 test ("LD" stands for "lethal dose") is a classic example of an exposure-response test. A measure of acute lethality, the test was developed in the 1920's to determine the potency of digitalis and other medicinal preparations derived from biological materials. It provides a statistically accurate measure of the amount of a chemical that will produce 50 percent mortality in a population of animals, that is, the amount of the chemical that will kill half of them. Comparison of LD50 values for different agents gives a measure of relative toxicity. A variation on the LD50 test is the ED50 (for "effective dose"), which measures the amount of a chemical that will produce a deleterious effect other than death in 50 percent of the population.

The Draize ocular- and skin-irritation tests are other classic indexes that are widely used today. John H. Draize of the Food and Drug Administration standardized the protocol for the ocular-irritation test in the 1940's; it dictates specific procedures for measuring eye irritation in rabbits. A fixed dose of a chemical (.1 milliliter of a liquid or .1 gram of a solid) is placed in one of a rabbit's eyes; the other eye serves as a control. For the skin test, an area of the rabbit's hide is shaved and covered with the chemical being tested. In both tests there is a specific set of criteria for scoring irritation and inflammation.

The LD50 test and the Draize tests are probably the toxicity tests most familiar to the public; they are also the ones singled out most frequently by animal-welfare activists. But chemicals are usually screened through many additional in vivo tests. These include acute toxicity tests other than the LD50 and subchronic and chronic toxicity tests that last anywhere from two weeks to two years. Such tests provide information on mechanisms of action, target organs, symptomatology and carcinogenicity (the ability to cause cancer) as well as lethality.

Other tests help to fill out the toxic profile of a chemical. Reproductive and developmental toxicity tests evaluate chemicals' effects on reproductive success and their ability to cause developmental malformations, a property known as teratogenicity. Hypersensitivity procedures test for chemicals that may not directly damage the skin but may elicit instead an immunological response similar to the one produced by poison ivy. Phototoxicity testing determines whether sunlight will activate a test chemical and thus enhance skin irritation.

Studies of toxicokinetics are sometimes carried out to trace the absorption, distribution, metabolism, storage and excretion of a chemical. Such studies are quite useful when the same chemical exhibits differences in toxicokinetics in two animal species. Finally, neurological and behavioral tests monitor the effects of chemicals on cognitive functions in adult animals as well as in developing fetuses.

It is probably clear from this recitation of procedures that complete toxicological evaluation of even one chemical is complicated, time-consuming and expensive. Testing a typical new chemical costs between $500,000 and $1.5 million, takes up to two or three years and may entail the sacrifice of thousands of animals. Furthermore, tens of thousands of products already on the market have never been tested thoroughly. The National Academy of Sciences observed recently that many of those substances might not have been evaluated at all.

Obviously, enormous benefits would accrue from toxicity tests that are cheaper and faster than in vivo testing. Just as obviously, researchers will be hard-pressed to come up with a battery of in vitro tests that can match the exhaustive screening possible with whole-animal procedures. Workers are making progress on roughly half a dozen categories of techniques.

The area of in vitro testing that has been pursued the longest and has been the best funded is that of genotoxicity: the ability of a chemical to damage genetic material. Genotoxicity encompasses substances that cause cancer, gene mutation and chromosomal abnormalities. Whole-animal tests for carcinogenicity are among the most expensive and time-consuming toxicity tests, which is probably why more than $70 million has been spent in the U.S. over the past decade to find in vitro alternatives. The in vitro tests currently available, such as the standard Ames bacterial assay, are widely used to screen for potential genotoxicity, but they cannot be expected to preempt whole-animal tests of chronic exposure, such as the rodent lifetime bioassay.

Another area of in vitro testing that has a relatively long history is cytotoxicity testing. Simply put, cytotoxicity assays evaluate the ability of a substance to kill cells. Some of these assays were developed for special purposes, such as screening drugs for the ability to kill cancer cells; others are meant for more general use. The number of methods available for distinguishing dead cells from live cells has increased rapidly in the past several years. In fact, the limiting factor on cytotoxicity testing is the number of cell types that can be cultured in vitro.

Two test systems have received considerable attention in the context of in vitro cytotoxicity testing: the total cellular-protein assay and the neutral-red uptake assay. In both tests cells cultured in plastic petri dishes are treated with various concentrations of a test chemical added to the culture medium. After 24 hours of exposure, the test chemical is washed out of the medium and an analytical reagent is added. In the case of the total cellular-protein test a reagent called kenacid blue is added to the medium and reacts with proteins in the cells, imparting a blue color whose density can be measured. Healthy, rapidly growing cells contain more protein than dead ones: consequently, control cultures will be dark blue. Dishes in which cells have been killed by the test chemical will be progressively lighter in tone.

The concentration of the test chemical that produces 50 percent inhibition of protein content, known as the IC50, can be determined from the colors of the cell cultures and compared with the IC50's of known chemical toxins in order to rank the test chemical's relative toxicity. This assay can be automated to speed testing, and it can be performed in combination with enzymes that metabolize drugs so that the effects of chemical intermediates can be tested as well.

The assay measuring neutral-red uptake is not too different. Developed in its present form at Rockefeller University, the test is based on neutral red, a dye that is taken up from the culture medium and stored by living cells but not by dead ones. The amount of dye retained by the cells is an indication of the number of living cells. Again, an IC50 for the test chemical is established by linking cell mortality to the amount of the chemical the cells received. The assay is then quantified by comparing the IC50 with the IC50's of known toxins.

Although they may have only limited ability to predict tissue-specific effects or effects resulting from tissue or organ interactions, cytotoxicity tests do provide essential information on the intrinsic toxicity of pure chemicals, mixtures and formulations. They can also be fairly good indicators of ocular irritation, because cell death is a major cause of it. Corneal epithelial cells can be subjected to cytotoxicity testing for ocular irritation, and in fact, such tests are already used in product safety evaluation.

The Center for Alternatives to Animal Testing at Johns Hopkins University has identified more than 30 other in vitro tests that could be appropriate for testing ocular irritation. Some of these also test for cytotoxicity, but others have different end points. Ray Tchao of the Philadelphia College of Pharmacy and Science, for example, has devised a protocol to detect impairment of the so-called tight junctions between cells, junctions that are important in controlling the penetration of substances through the corneal epithelial cell layer.

The so-called CAM test, pioneered by Joseph Leighton of the Medical College of Pennsylvania and by Niels P. Lupke of the University of Münster, provides another in vitro measure of inflammation. In the CAM test, part of the shell of a fertilized chicken egg is carefully removed to reveal the delicate, veined chorioallantoic membrane (CAM) underneath. A test chemical is applied directly to the membrane; sometimes a Teflon ring is also placed on the membrane to contain the chemical. Researchers look for inflammation of the membrane five minutes and 24 hours after the chemical has been applied.

Several laboratories have also been exploring cultures of human epidermal cells as models of human skin. Some skin-cell culture methods are descended from skin-regeneration techniques developed for burn patients. The skin-cell cultures can be tested for inflammation much as the membrane in a CAM test is. Measuring the biological response to chemicals, however, is easier in skin-cell cultures than it is in CAM tests.

In vitro tests are also being developed to monitor toxicity in particular target organs. The question of target-organ toxicity is answered in vivo by examining the organs of a treated animal for pathological changes. In vitro, cells from specific organs must be cultured and tested. Considerable progress has been made on in vitro screening for liver, blood, heart, kidney, lung and nervous-system toxicity.

The techniques for culturing hepatocytes (liver cells) are particularly well developed. Methods of in vitro hepatotoxicity testing, derived from experiments in liver research, involve isolated liver cells, liver slices and isolated, perfused whole livers. Human hepatocytes have already been used in some tests; where the cells of other animals are used instead, in vitro target-organ data can still reduce substantially the number of animals needed for conclusive results. Enough tissue can be obtained from two or three animals to conduct studies that would ordinarily require from 20 to 40 animals.

The purpose of these in vitro systems ranges from identifying chemicals that specifically produce toxicity in the liver to determining the metabolic kinetics of chemicals and the way in which they are excreted. Test systems based on rat hepatocytes can also evaluate cellular markers for potential toxicity. As more knowledge is obtained about the mechanisms of toxic action of chemicals in organ systems, new in vitro methods can be developed to test for these effects.

Progress has also been made in identifying in vitro systems for evaluating teratogenicity. The key to teratogenicity testing lies in establishing the relation between in vitro indexes of toxicological response and the complex process of differential toxicity in the developing organism, particularly in the human fetus. Although many of the alternative test systems proposed involve whole organisms—from the hydra or fruit fly to frog or rodent embryos—and therefore circumvent the problem of extrapolation between cell cultures and whole animals, the systems still have significant problems in predicting human teratogenicity.

In some cases, mathematical and computer models may be able to supplement the information provided by in vitro testing. Mathematical pharmacokinetic models are already helping toxicologists to estimate in vivo toxicokinetics from in vitro data. Computer-based "structure-activity" analyses attempt to correlate general toxicological responses with aspects of the molecular structure of the test chemical. Such methods are currently empirical, but they should improve as specific mechanisms of interaction are related to chemical structure.

The complexity of the exposure-response relationship seems, however, to rule out the possibility of making sound predictions from theoretical principles alone. The response of an organism to a given exposure of a chemical results from a diffuse array of interdependent processes at the molecular, cellular and organismal levels. In addition to the absorption, distribution, metabolism, storage and excretion of substances described by toxicokinetics, the outcome of an organism's exposure to a chemical also depends on toxicodynamics.

Toxicodynamics has to do with alterations in the biological system that are a consequence of the presence of a chemical in the system. At the molecular level such alterations are biochemical: they can, for example, inhibit an enzyme critical to normal cellular function. At higher levels of organization the alterations are manifested as tissue pathology or as clinical toxicity.

If a human being is exposed to a chemical, the toxicokinetic properties of the chemical determine whether the agent or one of its metabolites will ultimately reach a sensitive cellular or molecular target and initiate a biological response. If the reactive form of the chemical does reach the potential target, the toxicodynamics determine to what degree the agent will adversely affect the human being. The ultimate expression of pathology depends on the human organism's ability to repair toxin-induced damage at all levels of biological organization: the molecular and cellular levels as well as the levels of organs and tissues.

The toxicokinetics and toxicodynamics of a chemical and the ability of a biological system to effect repair all come to bear on the exposure-response relationship. It is easy to see why it is challenging to predict human toxicity with anything short of a whole organism. Indeed, current predictive toxicology draws not just from whole-animal experiments and theory but from a historical data base, compiled over years of experience, that relates the results of in vivo testing to human epidemiological data and even in some cases to the outcome of accidental human exposure.

The foregoing discussion of toxicokinetic and toxicodynamic interactions underscores the most obvious and important advantage of whole-animal testing: it provides an integrated biological system that serves as a surrogate for the complexities of human and other animal systems. In vivo tests have several other features that must be reckoned with. They can be used to assess the outcome of exposure by different routes (whether through ingestion, contact with the skin or inhalation) and over long periods (chronic toxicity tests can take a year or longer). In addition, whole-animal studies can be designed to determine whether or not particular toxic effects are reversible—an important parameter in risk assessment and risk management.

How might in vitro testing provide the same information? Would it be necessary to have one in vitro test for every potential target-cell type in the body? How can in vitro tests evaluate toxicological responses that involve, say, immunological processes or blood pressure? How can they evaluate chronic toxicity or recovery from toxic insults? How can exposure by ingestion, inhalation or topical contact be simulated? These problems must be solved if in vitro tests are ever to replace in vivo testing completely.

Another potential stumbling block concerns the testing of human-cell cultures, which, because it would eliminate the need for species extrapolation, is billed as one of the benefits of in vitro testing. There are a few hitches. Currently not all human cell types can be cultured; some types of cells "dedifferentiate" in vitro, that is, they take on the qualities of primitive, unspecialized cells instead of retaining the characteristics that identify them as muscle cells, spleen cells, colon cells and so on. Furthermore, the supply of normal human cells available for toxicological testing is somewhat limited. In order for human cells to be routinely employed in toxicity testing, some means of making them more readily available must be found.

These obstacles should be weighed against the disadvantages of whole-animal testing that we have already mentioned: animal discomfort and death, species-extrapolation problems and excessive time and expense. In vitro tests could ameliorate all of these problems and several more. For example, whereas whole-animal testing is hard to standardize, the standardization of in vitro techniques is fairly straightforward. Furthermore, the dose of a chemical that is received by each cultured cell can be measured and controlled with precision, making it easier to establish the critical concentrations of toxins. Because much smaller quantities of a substance can be used, novel compounds available in limited amounts can be tested, and disposal problems are minimized if a compound turns out to be toxic.

It takes time to overcome the problems inherent in introducing any new technology. It also takes time to gain acceptance for a new technology when the incumbent technology can boast a 50- to 60-year record of empirical findings. Before any new in vitro test can become a regular, routine source of toxicological data, it will have to be validated. That means it must be shown to be reliable (to give consistent results in different laboratories and at different times in the same laboratory) and meaningful (to provide information that contributes to chemical safety evaluation). To promote acceptance, toxicologists must also begin to compile data bases for in vitro tests so that better predictions can be drawn from the results.

Contrary to a prevailing misperception, in vitro tests need not replace existing in vivo test procedures in order to be useful. They can contribute to chemical safety evaluation right now. In vitro tests, for example, can be incorporated into the earliest stages of the risk-assessment process; they can be used to identify chemicals having the lowest probability of toxicity so that animals need be exposed only to less noxious chemicals. Such a procedure would reduce the number of animals tested and would also save time and the expense of research and development for products likely to fail subsequent safety evaluations. It is encouraging to note that several corporations have already implemented this approach in their testing strategies.

In any case, insisting on comprehensive replacement of existing tests will only delay the implementation of in vitro methods indefinitely. In vitro toxicity testing will not replace animal testing in a single, quantum step. In fact, regulatory mechanisms do not yet exist for review and approval of new in vitro testing methodologies for chemical safety evaluation. With time, in vitro testing will become more firmly established, and it will eventually play a critical role in the safety-evaluation process. It is our hope that this goal will be attained with the support and encouragement of industry, regulatory agencies, the scientific community and animal-welfare advocates alike.

A PLEA FOR THE CHIMPS[7]

The chimpanzee is more like us, genetically, than any other animal. It is because of similarities in physiology, in biochemistry, in the immune system, that medical science makes use of the living bodies of chimpanzees in its search for cures and vaccines for a variety of human diseases.

There are also behavioral, psychological and emotional similarities between chimpanzees and humans, resemblances so striking that they raise a serious ethical question: are we justified in using an animal so close to us—an animal, moreover, that is highly endangered in its African forest home—as a human substitute in medical experimentation?

In the long run, we can hope that scientists will find ways of exploring human physiology and disease, and of testing cures and vaccines, that do not depend on the use of living animals of any sort. A number of steps in this direction already have been taken, prompted in large part by a growing public awareness of the suffering that is being inflicted on millions of animals. More and more people are beginning to realize that nonhuman animals—even rats and guinea pigs—are not just unfeeling machines but are capable of enjoying their lives, and of feeling fear, pain and despair.

But until alternatives have been found, medical science will continue to use animals in the battle against human disease and suffering. And some of those animals will continue to be chimpanzees.

Because they share with us 99 percent of their genetic material, chimpanzees can be infected with some human diseases that do not infect other animals. They are currently being used in research on the nature of hepatitis non-A non-B, for example, and they continue to play a major role in the development of vaccines against hepatitis B.

Many biomedical laboratories are looking to the chimpanzee to help them in the race to find a vaccine against acquired immune deficiency syndrome. Chimpanzees are not good models

[7]Reprint of an article by primatologist Jane Goodall, director of the Gombe Stream Research Center, Tanzania. *New York Times Magazine.* My 17 '87. pp 108+.
Copyright 1987 by the New York Times Company. Reprinted with permission.

for AIDS research; although the AIDS virus stays alive and replicates within the chimpanzee's bloodstream, no chimp has yet come down with the disease itself. Nevertheless, many of the scientists involved argue that only by using chimpanzees can potential vaccines be safely tested.

Given the scientists' professed need for animals in research, let us turn aside from the sensitive ethical issue of whether chimpanzees *should* be used in medical research, and consider a more immediate issue: how are we treating the chimpanzees that are actually being used?

Just after Christmas I watched, with shock, anger and anguish, a videotape—made by an animal-rights group during a raid—revealing the conditions in a large biomedical research laboratory, under contract to the National Institutes of Health, in which various primates, including chimpanzees, are maintained. In late March, I was given permission to visit the facility.

It was a visit I shall never forget. Room after room was lined with small, bare cages, stacked one above the other, in which monkeys circled round and round and chimpanzees sat huddled, far gone in depression and despair.

Young chimpanzees, 3 or 4 years old, were crammed, two together, into tiny cages measuring 22 inches by 22 inches and only 24 inches high. They could hardly turn around. Not yet part of any experiment, they had been confined in these cages for more than three months.

The chimps had each other for comfort, but they would not remain together for long. Once they are infected, probably with hepatitis, they will be separated and placed in another cage. And there they will remain, living in conditions of severe sensory deprivation, for the next several years. During that time, they will become insane.

A juvenile female rocked from side to side, sealed off from the outside world behind the glass doors of her metal isolation chamber. She was in semidarkness. All she could hear was the incessant roar of air rushing through vents into her prison.

In order to demonstrate the "good" relationship the lab's caretaker had with this chimpanzee, one of the scientists told him to lift her from the cage. The caretaker opened the door. She sat, unmoving. He reached in. She did not greet him—nor did he greet her. As if drugged, she allowed him to take her out. She sat motionless in his arms. He did not speak to her, she did not look at him. He touched her lips briefly. She did not respond. He returned her to her cage. She sat again on the bars of the floor. The door closed.

I shall be haunted forever by her eyes, and by the eyes of the other infant chimpanzees I saw that day. Have you ever looked into the eyes of a person who, stressed beyond endurance, has given up, succumbed utterly to the crippling helplessness of despair? I once saw a little African boy, whose whole family had been killed during the fighting in Burundi. He too looked out at the world, unseeing, from dull, blank eyes.

Though this particular laboratory may be one of the worst, from what I have learned, most of the other biomedical animal-research facilities are not much better. Yet only when one has some understanding of the true nature of the chimpanzee can the cruelty of these captive conditions be fully understood.

Chimpanzees are very social by nature. Bonds between individuals, particularly between family members and close friends, can be affectionate, supportive, and can endure throughout their lives. The accidental separation of two friendly individuals may cause them intense distress. Indeed, the death of a mother may be such a psychological blow to her child that even if the child is 5 years old and no longer dependent on its mother's milk, it may pine away and die.

It is impossible to overemphasize the importance of friendly physical contact for the well-being of the chimpanzee. Again and again one can watch a frightened or tense individual relax if she is patted, kissed or embraced reassuringly by a companion. Social grooming, which provides hours of close contact, is undoubtedly the single most important social activity.

Chimpanzees in their natural habitat are active for much of the day. They travel extensively within their territory, which can be as large as 50 square kilometers for a community of about 50 individuals. If they hear other chimpanzees calling as they move through the forest, or anticipate arriving at a good food source, they typically break into excited charging displays, racing along the ground, hurling sticks and rocks and shaking the vegetation. Youngsters, particularly, are full of energy, and spend long hours playing with one another or by themselves, leaping through the branches and gamboling along the ground. Adults sometimes join these games. Bunches of fruit, twigs and rocks may be used as toys.

Chimpanzees enjoy comfort. They construct sleeping platforms each night, using a multitude of leafy twigs to make their beds soft. Often, too, they make little "pillows" on which to rest during a midday siesta.

Chimps are highly intelligent. They display cognitive abilities that were, until recently, thought to be unique to humans. They are capable of cross-model transfer of information—that is, they can identify by touch an object they previously have only seen, and vice versa. They are capable of reasoned thought, generalization, abstraction and symbolic representation. They have some concept of self. They have excellent memories and can, to some extent, plan for the future. They show a capacity for intentional communication that depends, in part, on their ability to understand the motives of the individuals with whom they are communicating.

Chimpanzees are capable of empathy and altruistic behavior. They show emotions that are undoubtedly similar, if not identical, to human emotions—joy, pleasure, contentment, anxiety, fear and rage. They even have a sense of humor.

The chimpanzee child and the human child are alike in many ways: in their capacity for endless romping and fun; their curiosity; their ability to learn by observation, imitation and practice; and, above all, in their need for reassurance and love. When young chimpanzees are brought up in a human home and treated like human children, they learn to eat at table, to help themselves to snacks from the refrigerator, to sort and put away cutlery, to brush their teeth, to play with dolls, to switch on the television and select a program that interests them and watch it.

Young chimpanzees can easily learn over 200 signs of the American language of the deaf and use these signs to communicate meaningfully with humans and with one another. One youngster, in the laboratory of Dr. Roger S. Fouts, a psychologist at Central Washington University, has picked up 68 signs from four older signing chimpanzee companions, with no human teaching. The chimp uses the signs in communication with other chimpanzees and with humans.

The chimpanzee facilities in most biomedical research laboratories allow for the expression of almost none of these activities and behaviors. They provide little—if anything—more than the warmth, food and water, and veterinary care required to sustain life. The psychological and emotional needs of these creatures are rarely catered to, and often not even acknowledged.

In most labs the chimpanzees are housed individually, one chimp to a cage, unless they are part of a breeding program. The standard size of each cage is about 25 feet square and about 6 feet high. In one facility, a cage described in the catalogue as "large," designed for a chimpanzee of up to 25 kilograms (55 pounds), measures 2 feet 6 inches by 3 feet 8 inches, with a height of 5 feet 4 inches. Federal requirements for cage size are dependent on body size; infant chimpanzees, who are the most active, are often imprisoned in the smallest cages.

In most labs, the chimpanzees cannot even lie with their arms and legs outstretched. They are not let out to exercise. There is seldom anything for them to do other than eat, and then only when food is brought. The caretakers are usually too busy to pay much attention to individual chimpanzees. The cages are bleak and sterile, with bars above, bars below, bars on every side. There is no comfort in them, no bedding. The chimps, infected with human diseases, will often feel sick and miserable.

What of the human beings who administer these facilities—the caretakers, veterinarians and scientists who work at them? If they are decent, compassionate people, how can they condone, or even tolerate, the kind of conditions I have described?

They are, I believe, victims of a system that was set up long before the cognitive abilities and emotional needs of chimpanzees were understood. Newly employed staff members, equipped with a normal measure of compassion, may well be sickened by what they see. And, in fact, many of them do quit their jobs, unable to endure the suffering they see inflicted on the animals yet feeling powerless to help.

But others stay on and gradually come to accept the cruelty, believing (or forcing themselves to believe) that it is an inevitable part of the struggle to reduce human suffering. Some become hard and callous in the process, in Shakespeare's words, "all pity choked with custom of fell deeds."

A handful of compassionate and dedicated caretakers and veterinarians are fighting to improve the lots of the animals in their care. Vets are often in a particularly difficult position, for if they stand firm and try to uphold high standards of humane care, they will not always be welcome in the lab.

Many of the scientists believe that a bleak, sterile and restricting environment is necessary for their research. The cages must be small, the scientists maintain, because otherwise it is too diffi-

cult to treat the chimpanzees—to inject them, to draw their blood
or to anesthetize them. Moreover, they are less likely to hurt
themselves in small cages.

The cages must also be barren, with no bedding or toys, say
the scientists. This way, the chimpanzees are less likely to pick up
diseases or parasites. Also, if things are lying about, the cages are
harder to clean.

And the chimpanzees must be kept in isolation, the scientists
believe, to avoid the risk of cross-infection, particularly in hepatitis research.

Finally, of course, bigger cages, social groups and elaborate
furnishings require more space, more caretakers—and more
money. Perhaps, then, if we are to believe these researchers, it is
not possible to improve conditions for chimpanzees imprisoned
in biomedical research laboratories.

I believe not only that it *is* possible, but that improvements are
absolutely necessary. If we do not do something to help these
creatures, we make a mockery of the whole concept of justice.

Perhaps the most important way we can improve the quality of
life for the laboratory chimps is to increase the number of carefully trained caretakers. These people should be selected for their
understanding of animal behavior and their compassion and respect for, and dedication to, their charges. Each caretaker, having
established a relationship of trust with the chimpanzees in his
care, should be allowed to spend time with the animals over and
above that required for cleaning the cages and providing the
animals with food and water.

It has been shown that a chimpanzee who has a good relationship with his caretaker will cooperate calmly during experimental procedures, rather than react with fear or anger. At the
Dutch Primate Research Center, at Rijswijk, for example, some
chimpanzees have been trained to leave their group cage on com-
mand and move into small, single cages for treatment. At the
Stanford Primate Center in California, a number of chimpanzees
were taught to extend their arms for the drawing of blood. In
return they were given a food reward.

Much can be done to alleviate the pain and stress felt by
younger chimpanzees during experimental procedures. A youngster, for example, can be treated when in the presence of a trusted
human friend. Experiments have shown that young chimps react
with high levels of distress if subjected to mild electric shocks

when alone, but show almost no fear or pain when held by a sympathetic caretaker.

What about cage size? Here we should emulate the animal protection regulations that already exist in Switzerland. These laws stipulate that a cage must be, at minimum, about 20 meters square and 3 meters high for pairs of chimpanzees.

The chimpanzees should never be housed alone unless this is an essential part of the experimental procedure. For chimps in solitary confinement, particularly youngsters, three to four hours of friendly interaction with a caretaker should be mandatory. A chimp taking part in hepatitis research, in which the risk of cross-infection is, I am told, great, can be provided with a companion of a compatible species if it doesn't infringe on existing regulations—a rhesus monkey, for example, which cannot catch or pass on the disease.

For healthy chimpanzees there should be little risk of infection from bedding and toys. Stress and depression, however, can have deleterious effects on their health. It is known that clinically depressed humans are more prone to a variety of physiological disorders, and heightened stress can interfere with immune function. Given the chimpanzee's similarities to humans, it is not surprising that the chimp in a typical laboratory, alone in his bleak cage, is an easy prey to infections and parasites.

Thus, the chimpanzees also should be provided with a rich and stimulating environment. Climbing apparatus should be obligatory. There should be many objects for them to play with or otherwise manipulate. A variety of simple devices designed to alleviate boredom could be produced quite cheaply. Unexpected food items will elicit great pleasure. If a few simple buttons in each cage were connected to a computer terminal, it would be possible for the chimpanzees to feel they at least have some control over their world—if one button produced a grape when pressed, another a drink, or another a video picture. (The Canadian Council of Animal Care recommends the provision of television for primates in solitary confinement, or other means of enriching their environment.)

Without doubt, it will be considerably more costly to maintain chimpanzees in the manner I have outlined. Should we begrudge them the extra dollars? We take from them their freedom, their health and often their lives. Surely, the least we can do is try to provide them with some of the things that could make their imprisonment more bearable.

There are hopeful signs. I was immensely grateful to officials of the National Institutes of Health for allowing me to visit the primate facility, enabling me to see the conditions there and judge them for myself. And I was even more grateful for the fact that they gave me a great deal of time for serious discussions of the problem. Doors were opened and a dialogue begun. All who were present at the meetings agreed that, in light of present knowledge, it is indeed necessary to give chimpanzees a better deal in the labs.

Plans are now under way for a major conference to discuss ways and means of bringing about such change. Sponsored by the N.I.H. and organized by Roger Fouts (who toured the lab with me) and myself, this conference—which will be held in mid-December at the Jane Goodall Institute in Tucson, Ariz.—will bring together for the first time administrators, scientists and animal technicians from various primate facilities around the country and from overseas. The conference will, we hope, lead to the formulation of new, humane standards for the maintenance of chimpanzees in the laboratory.

I have had the privilege of working among wild, free chimpanzees for more than 26 years. I have gained a deep understanding of chimpanzee nature. Chimpanzees have given me so much in my life. The least I can do is to speak out for the hundreds of chimpanzees who, right now, sit hunched, miserable and without hope, staring out with dead eyes from their metal prisons. They cannot speak for themselves.

III. THE MOVEMENT IN TRANSITION

EDITOR'S INTRODUCTION

Most people in the United States lived and worked closely with animals until a few generations ago, when city and suburban life became the norm. For the most part, we no longer need horses and mules for transportation, our yards are free of goats and chickens, and we do not make our own clothes out of home-grown wool. But we still depend on animals, albeit indirectly, and the animal-based industries that serve us are worth billions of dollars annually and employ many thousands of people.

Historically, Americans have been reluctant to renounce a particular use of animals unless two conditions are met: There is a general sense of outrage over the use, and there is a good, cheap, readily available alternative. Such is the case with fur, which has been steadily losing ground in the United States in recent years, as Jeanie Kasindorf describes in the first article in this section, reprinted from *New York* magazine. The attack on fur has been so successful that in the spring of 1991 the Hudson's Bay Company announced its intention to shut down a fur-selling operation that had been in existence for some 300 years.

More animals are killed each year for food than for medical research, and most of them are raised on automated "factory farms" which bear little resemblance to the farms of the past. The second selection, Richard Conniff's article "Superchicken," describes how the modern poultry industry operates, using methods that involve overcrowded cages, mass suffocation, outbreaks of disease, and long-term stress. Next Michael Satchell's article reports on recent confrontations between animal advocates and hunters.

In the United States, there are now several thousand animal-welfare and animal-protection organizations. They include traditional animal shelters and lost-pet services, companies that sell cosmetics and household cleaners that have not been tested on animals, vegetarian societies, wildlife conservation groups, and interventionist groups like the International Fund for Animal Welfare and Greenpeace, which send teams all over the world to rescue abused or threatened animals. Many of the people who belong to these organizations have links with other reform movements, including environmentalism, pacificism, feminism, and the human-rights movement. Macdonald Daly, in the fourth selection in this section, recounts the origins of the antivivisection movement in Victorian England, its alliance with women suffragists and trade unionists, and its support by eminent writers such as Thomas Hardy and George Bernard Shaw.

Like all reform movements, the animal-rights movement has its inevitable blind spots, inconsistencies, and hypocrisies. Richard Conniff, in "Fuzzy-Wuzzy Thinking About Animal Rights," skewers the tendency of many animal lovers to romanticize animals—the ultimate "noble savages"—and to impose human ideals of justice and morality on a world in which suffering is normal and natural. Nonetheless, despite charges of fanaticism and ignorance, and despite massive opposition from the vested interests that would lose money if the idea of animal rights gained legitimacy, the movement is growing and has had notable successes in recent years. Merritt Clifton describes some of them, and looks at the future of the movement in America and across the globe, in "Out of the Cage: The Movement in Transition."

THE FUR FLIES[1]

"A couple of Sundays before Christmas, I was lunching at Mortimer's with Marietta Tree," says author Cleveland Amory, who founded the Fund for Animals in 1967. "And we had a knock-down-drag-out about her mink coat. She's an old and dear friend, and she said to me, 'If they're ranched, it's all right.' And I said, 'No, Marietta, it's not all right.' Another guy there even turned against me. He said, 'My mother had leopard coats and we knew we couldn't get away with wearing them, so we made them into suitcases.' Can you imagine what I was doing there with this guy? The night before that, I saw Alice Topping at a party, and

[1]Reprint of an article by Jeanie Kasindorf. *New York*. 23:26–33. Ja 15, '90. Copyright 1990 by News America Publishing, Inc. All rights reserved. Reprinted with the permission of *New York* Magazine.

she said to me, 'I'd sue anybody who sprayed my coat, Cleveland. I don't care what you believe.' "

Welcome to the new upscale urban war zone. All around the city this winter, you can hear the sounds of men and women fighting over fur coats. On 42nd Street, a cloth-coat-clad woman walks by a woman wearing a full-length mink. "A hundred animals were murdered for that coat," she yells out as she strides quickly by. "I hope you're happy wearing it."

On a subway train to Brooklyn, a women in a beaver coat sits down next to a young woman with a FUR HURTS button pinned to her lapel. As she does, she brushes against her face. "Keep your dead animals to yourself," the woman tells her.

On Park Avenue, a young woman in a raincoat passes a handsome salt-and-pepper-haired woman wearing a long silver-fox coat. "You assh--- with those furs!" the young woman yells. The woman in the silver fox spins around. "It's none of your goddamned f--- ing business!" she screams down Park Avenue. The woman in the raincoat turns and gives her new antagonist the finger.

At first glance, there is something riotously funny about these scenes from the fur wars. If they did not exist, "Doonesbury" cartoonist Garry Trudeau—who has drawn several strips about the controversy—would surely have invented them. But to the men and women on either side, there is nothing comic about this fight. To the animal-rights activists (who look at a fox coat and see 50 dead foxes), this is a battle to save the lives of millions of animals. To the furriers (who have watched in horror as sales in the Netherlands dropped 90 percent), this is a struggle for a business that is their life.

The fight against fur coats has been waged for a long time. "The first time I ever did a broadcast about fur coats was in 1965," says Cleveland Amory, "at the New York World's Fair. I was being interviewed by Barbara Walters, and when I began talking about fur coats, she was just amazed. She said, 'Cleveland, do you really think you're going to stop women in America from wearing furs?' And I said, 'Barbara, I'm sure as hell going to try.' I said, 'We're going to try to make them relate the coat on their back to the cruelty involved in making it.' "

But it was not until the late eighties that the fur fight escalated, fueled by the street warfare that was being used successfully by activists in Europe. In New York—where one third of all the fur

coats in America are sold—demonstrators began holding an annual march down Fifth Avenue on the day after Thanksgiving,
which they dubbed "Fur-Free Friday." They demonstrated in
front of department stores that sold furs. Some wrote MURDERER
in red paint on the sidewalk in front of the Fur Vault. They
started confronting fur wearers on the street. And they began
using actresses like Daryl Hannah and Kim Basinger to try to
convince American women that it was no longer smart and sexy to
wear fur.

For several years, the fur industry ignored the activists. "We
hoped that if we did not respond," says Tom Riley, the vice-presi-
dent of the Fur Information Council of America, "it would become a nonevent." But last fall, the council realized it could ignore the issue no longer. Sales were suffering. The three publicly
traded fur companies—Antonovich, Evans, and the Fur Vault—
were reporting losses.

The fur industry decided that it had to fight back. It launched
a multi-million-dollar public-relations and advertising campaign
against the activists, trying to convince the public that the battle
over fur was the first step in a plan by wild-eyed radicals to take
away every American's right to use animals for food, clothing,
even medical research. As the decade began, it looked as if the fur
wars would be with us for a long time to come.

"One of the reasons the movement has grown over the past
two years in New York City," says Steve Siegel, the New York
director of Trans-Species Unlimited, "is that we decided we
would have to be confrontational." Siegel is a media-savvy fund-
raiser and public-relations man (Tom Riley calls him a "terrorist")
whom Trans-Species hired to set up its New York office in 1987.
The organization, which deserves much of the credit for the
movement's success in the city, was founded in 1981 by a writing
teacher at Penn State. Trans-Species—in contrast to animal-protection groups such as the Humane Society of the United States—
is dedicated to eliminating all forms of animal exploitation.

Trans-Species held its first Fur-Free Friday in 1986. This past
November, more than 3,000 people were led down Fifth Avenue
from 59th Street to Madison Square Park at 25th Street by Bob
Barker, who resigned in 1987 as host of the Miss Universe and
Miss U.S.A. pageants when contest officials refused to stop
awarding fur coats as prizes. For the first time in the march's short

history, there were so many demonstrators that the police had to move them off the sidewalk and onto the street.

"Every other weekend after Fur-Free Friday," says Siegel, "we are out on the street in front of the Fur Vault or a store that sells furs. We also organize 'speak-outs' in which we send people out on Fifth Avenue and confront people and give them literature. We encourage our members to confront people wherever they are. We tell them to say whatever they want, to go right up to the point of legal harassment but not to harass them. We have lawyers who instruct our people how far they can go. If they use profanity or threaten or even follow somebody, that could be legal harassment, but anything up to that point is okay."

Many New Yorkers, like Alice Topping, believe that animal activists are walking up and down Fifth Avenue almost daily, throwing red paint at women in fur coats. It's one of the great myths of the fur wars—and each side blames the other for perpetuating it. Both Tom Riley and Steve Siegel say they have heard of it happening to only a couple of women in New York City.

The Police Department says it has received no reports of attacks against anyone wearing a fur coat during an organized demonstration in the city. The police do not keep computer records of individual incidents but officers in the 19th Precinct where confrontations would be most likely to occur, recall no such attacks.

Acts of violence have been committed against fur stores, however. Activists chained and padlocked the front door of the Fur Vault on Fifth Avenue near 47th Street one Saturday in 1985, locking employees and customers in the store for fifteen minutes. In Connecticut, someone walked into the Greenwich Hospital thrift shop in December, slashed the pelts on four fur coats, and left unnoticed. The Fur Vault in Westbury, Long Island, received a bomb threat one night the week before Christmas and had to empty the store. The police never found any explosives.

The worst acts of violence have been committed in other cities. Along Wisconsin Avenue in Bethesda, Maryland, just outside Washington, D.C., where there is a Fur Vault and a Saks Fifth Avenue, animal activists drive by a couple of times a year, shooting out windows with pellet guns and throwing red paint on the buildings. At an International Fur Mart sale in Detroit last winter, animal activists defaced 75 fur coats with razor blades and chewing gum and were never caught. In Santa Rosa, California, a fur store was set on fire one evening when it was empty. The fire destroyed the store as well as the fur coats that had not been stored in a vault for the night.

Street warfare is not the activists' only weapon. The organizations have also adopted the oldest tactic on Madison Avenue. They have signed up a long list of actresses and models to try to illustrate the beauty of *not* wearing fur. "In addition to relying on the moral argument," says Steve Siegel, "we decided we would also have to give selfish people a selfish reason to stop wearing fur. We decided to make fur seem vulgar, a symbol of someone who is tasteless and uneducated, so that people would feel they were being admired if they didn't wear fur."

The Humane Society persuaded *Vogue* model Carré Otis to appear in its "I'd be ashamed to wear fur" ad. People for the Ethical Treatment of Animals (PETA), another of the new aggressive animal-rights organizations, started campaigns this year that spoof Blackglama's famous tag line, "What Becomes a Legend Most?" The ads feature a picture of *Elvira* actress Cassandra Peterson draped in a mink, with the phrase "Fur Is Dead" scrawled across the coat. Above the photograph, the copy asks, "What Disgraces a Legend Most?"

Carol Burnett, who was once one of the Blackglama "Legends," says she has given away her fur coats. Kim Basinger, Rosanna Arquette, Ali MacGraw, Ally Sheedy, Daryl Hannah, Kirstie Alley, and the "Golden Girls"—Betty White, Bea Arthur, and Rue McClanahan—have taken a stand against wearing fur. Even some designers have joined in. Carolina Herrera and Bill Blass both said last year that "for personal reasons" they had decided not to design fur coats. When Giorgio Armani introduced a line of fake furs in Milan last March, the runway was crowded with stuffed toy animals while a voice over the loudspeaker said, "Thank you, Emporio Armani, for saving our skins." Now Stephen Sprouse has gotten into the act, announcing that he will soon unveil an "anti-fur coat."

Candice Bergen, who as Murphy Brown has become television's newest role model for the smart, successful working woman, has also lent her name to the Humane Society campaign. "I was given a mink coat when I was 21," she says, "and I gave it away then. I've been concerned about this issue for twenty years, but there was just never a receptive public. Lately, people have acquired an enormous consciousness about it. I think it's all in line with the concern for the environment, which is very hopeful.

There are a lot of people I know who have been approached to do those Blackglama ads who would no longer consider doing them. I have always refused to wear fur coats when I model. And the only time I wore one as an actress was in *Rich and Famous*, when I played a woman who was totally self-absorbed."

The campaign has been so successful that it is hard to find a celebrity who will publicly support fur. "The celebrity who speaks out will get 6,000 to 10,000 letters," says Tom Riley, "and they're not anxious to have that kind of machine against them."

The only celebrity the fur council has found to go public is former Olympic skier Suzy Chaffee, who helped design a collection of fur-lined outdoorwear (Suzy Chaffee Sport Furs). But she is likely to do little to help the campaign. "A lot of people don't want me to talk to the press 'cause they say they'll make a clown out of you," she says. "But my credibility is very important to me, and I feel I am really being responsible to the animals and to nature and to the environment, because trapping them is better than letting them die the disease-and-starvation route. I mean, it's like tough love. It would be sweet if you didn't have to kill anything, but they have to survive, we have to survive, and I think that's the price of it. I wish the animal-rights extremists would give their fur coats to the homeless. The fur industry does it every year at Grand Central station, and it's one of the most inspiring things I've ever done. First, they thought we were nuts. Then the light started coming back into their eyes. There's nothing like curling up in a fur coat in a corner of Grand Central station and fighting the cold."

Animal activists dream of doing what their counterparts in Holland have done—creating an almost fur-free country. In the Netherlands, sales of fur are 10 percent of what they were in 1982, and there are now only 32 furriers in a country where there used to be 400. Anti-fur sentiment is so strong that furriers' children are sometimes taunted by classmates.

In Great Britain and Switzerland, fur sales have dropped 75 percent in the past five years. In West Germany, they have fallen more than 25 percent. In Canada, the third-largest producer of fur in the world, the income of fur ranchers and trappers decreased 20 percent from 1987 to 1988.

The United States has not been hit as hard. Fur sales, according to the industry's own figures, have remained at $1.8 billion since 1986. In order to keep that figure constant, however, prices have had to be slashed dramatically. During the height of the season this winter, fur stores were offering 40 and 50 percent off regular prices. The publicly held fur-store chains all reported losses in their last fiscal year. Fred "the Furrier" Schwartz, who founded the Fur Vault in 1976, resigned in October 1988 after a major reorganization of the company. In November 1989, the ailing company announced that it was looking for a buyer for its retail-fur division. Two weeks ago, Antonovich filed for protection from its creditors.

Furriers insist that the hard times are the result not of the animal activists but of warm winters and a slow economy. "It's absolute nonsense to say the animal-rights activists have anything to do with it," says Robert Miller, the president of the Fur Vault. "Do they also take credit for layoffs in the financial community since October 1987? Do they also take credit for very weak retail sales? The problems in the fur industry have a lot to do with overexpansion, coupled with two years of relatively mild winters and the slowdown in retailing in general."

Still, people in the industry feel threatened enough by the activists that they have decided to fight back. Last fall, they launched an estimated $2-million public-relations campaign to try to convince the American public that the activists want to take away their right to use animals for anything. At the heart of the campaign are print ads that say, "Today fur. Tomorrow leather. Then wool. Then meat. . . . After that, medical research. Even circuses and zoos." Furriers say some customers are clipping out the ads so they can wave them at animal activists if they are stopped on the street.

The industry has formed a Fur Farm Animal Welfare Coalition, which is dedicated to getting the message out that fur farmers are humane. It has given $50,000 in seed money to another group called Furbearers Unlimited, which will train trappers. Riley is also establishing a Standards Review Board of veterinarians and scientists to make sure that animals on fur farms are treated responsibly. "I see a day when we have tags on coats that would assure the consumer that these pelts came from farms that met specific standards," Riley says, "and, if it is wild fur, that they were trapped by certified trappers."

Most animals killed for their fur do not die pretty deaths. Mink, which are raised on fur ranches, receive what could be described as the kindest treatment: They are placed in a small chamber filled with carbon monoxide or carbon dioxide. Ranch foxes are killed by electrocution—held down by two men who place an electric clip on the animal's lip and a probe in its anus, which shoots a bolt of electricity through its body. Although the Fur Farm Animal Welfare Coalition has set guidelines that call for killing ranch foxes by lethal injection, it concedes that such a method is not always used. PETA, which has an investigative team that makes surprise visits to fur ranches, says that some of the small mom-and-pop operations also kill animals by putting them in an enclosed area and suffocating them with the exhaust from a pickup truck.

Most wild animals—beavers, coyotes, fishers, lynx, muskrat, nutrias, otters, raccoon, weasels, wolverines, sables, and wild foxes—are caught with steel-jaw leg-hold traps or body-gripping traps. The steel-jaw trap—which has been outlawed in more than 70 countries but not in the United States—is the most common. It clamps tightly around the animal's foot or leg. The traps for beavers, nutrias, muskrats, and otters are placed underwater, where the animals drown after they are caught. Other animals sometimes die from injury, exposure, or an attack by a predator before the trapper finds them. An animal's attempt to free itself from a trap often results in severe damage. Some animals even bite off their legs to escape. Others struggle so hard that they kill themselves. If an animal is alive when the trapper finds it, he will club its head with a hammer until it dies, crush the animal's chest and rib cage with his feet until it stops breathing, or shoot it.

The body-gripping traps are designed to catch the animal at the back of its neck and kill it instantly. "The common misconception is that these traps are brutal," says Gordon Batcheller of the New York State Bureau of Wildlife. "I take exception to that. A trained trapper can set a leg-hold trap so in most cases it doesn't injure an animal, and can set a body-gripping trap so it results in a quick kill." But animal activists say that's nonsense. "The animal has to enter the trap in exactly the right way," says Patricia Ragan, a research associate at the Humane Society, "and in the real world that just doesn't happen. We see cases of bodies crushed and backs broken. One particularly gruesome case came in to us from Denver last year where a Doberman wandered just to the edge of its own property, put its head in an 'instant kill' trap, and dragged itself to the owner's door while it slowly strangled."

A Humane Society study estimates that at least 23 percent of the animals found in traps were not meant to be caught, including many domestic dogs and cats. "We had a case that was reported to us recently from a family in Florida," says Ragan. "Their black Labrador was walking along a creek bed with its two teenage owners. Its tongue got caught in a leg-hold trap and was ripped from the animal. They had to euthanize their pet."

There are no federal laws that regulate the raising and trapping of fur-bearing animals, and only a handful of state ones (Wyoming, for example, requires that ranch animals be kept in "reasonable" cages). In some states, animal-rights organizations have tried to get laws enacted to regulate the fur industry, but they have never gotten them out of legislative committee.

Every state does have a general animal-cruelty law that makes it illegal to "cruelly" kill, beat, mutilate, or harm animals. But local prosecutors rarely enforce those laws unless someone mistreats a domestic pet or farm horses and cows. "I've been studying this issue for ten years," says David Favre, a professor at the Detroit College of Law. "And I can't remember a time that a prosecutor brought a case against a fur farmer."

As a result, animal-rights activists are attacking the legal issue another way. On February 13, 1990, residents of Aspen, Colorado, will vote on a city-council resolution that would ban the sale of all fur products (except those from cattle, sheep, and goats) within city limits. Even supporters of the measure say that the results may hinge on the issue of Aspen's future as much as on the issue of fur. [The resolution was defeated.]

"In Aspen in the seventies, you would never find anybody in a fur coat," says anti-fur activist Katharine Thalberg, a bookstore owner and the wife of Mayor Bill Stirling, who helped get the measure on the ballot. "There was always a lot of money in Aspen, but there was a great effort not to flaunt it. Now there are people here leading a very ostentatious life-style, and people who don't care about animals are supporting us because fur represents the changing life-style in Aspen."

Some opponents have countered by launching a recall campaign against the mayor and three members of the city council on the ground that they are spending too much time worrying about issues like fur when they should be dealing with issues like housing and transportation. "What the fur vote really boils down to is an infringement of our civil liberties," says Mark Kirkland, the president of Aspen's Concerned Citizens Coalition and the manager of the Revillon shop, one of four fur stores in Aspen. "We really deplore the attempt to legislate away people's freedom of choice."

No matter where the public debate is taking place, it invariably comes down to the same few points. At the top of the list is the Meat and Leather Issue. The favorite argument of the pro-fur forces is that the only people who have the right to take a stand against them are those who do not eat meat or chicken or wear leather. "Fur is the oldest material human beings have worn," says designer Karl Lagerfeld, who has not given up his line of fur coats. "If we do this, then we have to stop eating meat, no leather shoes, nothing. Then you're back to nature completely." That's why the fur industry has made the Meat and Leather Issue the centerpiece of its ad campaign and is even planning a celebrity-designer benefit for a Ronald McDonald House later this year.

Corollary to the Meat and Leather Issue is the Ranch Issue. "We feel that ranch animals are part of the agricultural cycle," says Tom Riley. "We believe man has the right to use animals for these purposes, provided he is treating these animals responsibly." Members of Riley's camp argue that the methods used to kill fur-bearing animals are no more cruel than those used in processing beef and chicken. (A veal calf, for instance, is chained in a small wooden stall so that it cannot walk or even turn around for its entire life and is fed nothing but a liquid formula. Cattle are rendered unconscious by a compression gun that shoots metal bolts against their foreheads; then each animal is hung upside down by one of its legs and moved through a slaughtering plant, where its throat is cut. Chickens also have their throats cut; some are hung up first, and their heads are run through a vat of electrified water to stun them.)

Animal activists reply by raising the Vanity Issue. "We think it's perfectly logical to eat meat and wear leather and be against fur," says Laura Chapin, a spokeswoman for the Humane Society. "Because there's a perfectly logical dividing line between human need and human vanity, and people choose fur coats only for human vanity. Whether or not you choose to eat meat or wear leather, the cruelty inflicted on a farm animal doesn't cancel out the cruelty inflicted on fur-bearing animals." The Vanity Issue is one of Bob Barker's favorites. "The only reason anyone wears a fur coat is to demonstrate affluence," he says. "I have suggested that instead of killing 50 or 60 minks, to walk into a restaurant and impress people, women just wear a chic cloth coat and pin $100 bills to it."

Which brings us to the Warmth Issue, the Ozone Issue, and the Wildlife Conservation Issue. "You can ask literally hundreds of thousands of men and women, and they will tell you there's nothing as warm as wearing fur," says Tom Riley. "They are not just wearing fur for vanity. It's an organic product that doesn't deplete the ozone layer like products made from petro-chemicals. And trapping would be here whether the fur industry was here or not, because it is necessary to control the population and keep disease from spreading among wild animals. It is often an easier death than letting an animal die from disease."

Animal activists argue just the opposite. "Any reputable wild-life biologist will tell you that wild animals regulate their own population," says Steve Siegel. "If they get enough food, they will give birth to a larger litter. If they don't, they will give birth to smaller litters. Trapping and hunting do not regulate population. They only stimulate the birthrate to get the maximum yields for the hunters and trappers who pay the license fees."

On a bone-chilling Saturday afternoon before Christmas, six-teen members of Friends of Animals stood behind blue police barricades in front of the Fifth Avenue Fur Vault and tried to talk women out of buying and wearing furs.

"The animals are raised in small metal cages and killed by anal electrocution," Rich Siegel, a singer and jazz pianist, called out through a bullhorn at a woman wearing a red fox coat. "It's not a pleasant thought when you're making your fashion statement, is it, lady"?

In the center of the line of protesters, two women held a large blue banner that read, PEACE ON EARTH BEGINS WITH YOUR WARD-ROBE. The other demonstrators held large posters with pho-tographs of animals. Beneath each picture, bold letters read, LET ME LIVE. In the middle of the sidewalk, a young woman who used to own a raccoon coat passed out a pamphlet called "It's Their World, Too."

"Thank you for not buying fur," Rich Siegel said over and over again. "Thank you for not patronizing this and other stores that sell fur garments. Hundreds of hours of torture and suffer-ing go into making every fur garment. We think once you have the facts, you'll make a more compassionate choice."

Most of the women wearing fur coats rushed by the protesters, refusing to join in the debate. "I love it," said one woman about her raccoon coat. "I don't talk," another woman in a mink said.

Only a few were willing to discuss the issue. "Man has taken animals since he came out of the cave," said a woman wearing a fake leopard coat because she doesn't believe in killing endangered species. "If it's farm-raised, that's all right with me." Another woman in a raccoon coat said, "Everybody has a right to do what they want. You're not hurting anybody. This is for survival."

Finally, toward the end of the two-hour demonstration, the protesters got through to their first fur-coat-clad lady. A tall, striking woman in a silver fox walked by with her husband, who tried to steer her quickly past the demonstrators. "Let them not wear fur coats if they want," he grumbled, "but they should leave us alone. Why should they say what we do?" His wife pulled back long enough to take a pamphlet from a young woman wearing a FUR HURTS button. She slowly turned the pamphlet over in her hand.

"To be honest with you," she said, "I've never thought about this before. But I might think twice about it now."

SUPERCHICKEN: WHOSE LIFE IS IT ANYWAY?[2]

Over the past 60 years the chicken has undergone a remarkable transformation. Once a common backyard sight, it has almost disappeared from the landscape. Once a Sunday night treat, it is now a weekday staple. Our fast-food society has turned chicken into parts in a bucket, into nuggets, snacks. The average American tucks away 60 pounds of chicken a year, not counting eggs. At the present rate, we may be eating more chicken than beef by the mid-1990s.

What's made the chicken cheap, abundant, and yet oddly invisible is a combination of science and commerce. (Farmers don't enter the picture much these days except as temporary caretakers of the birds.) The science—poultry science—is unglamorous, but its achievements have been spectacular. In my grandparents' day it took 16 weeks to raise a two-pound meat bird. Breeding was

[2]Reprint of an article by Richard Conniff. *Discover.* 9:32-6+. Je '88. Copyright 1988 by Discover Publications. Reprinted with permission.

seasonal (hence, spring chickens), and farmers took pride in producing chickens in time for frying on the Fourth of July. Now broilers reach a market size of just over four pounds in seven weeks, *year-round*. In the 1920s a hen laid 120 eggs per year; the average now is 250 and rising.

In 1923, when Mrs. Wilmer Steele of Ocean View, Delaware, began the broiler industry, she sold her first flock of squawking, fully feathered birds for 62 cents a pound, liveweight. This week my local supermarket is selling packaged, ready-to-cook chicken parts on special for 39 cents a pound. Chickens and the eggs they produce have become our cheapest and most abundant source of animal protein. Poultrymen like to say that no government program has done as much to make food available to the poor.

But critics have begun to question what progress has done to the chicken. Has industrialization gone too far? By manipulating the chicken, even down to the bacteria that grow in its gut, are we turning it into a mechanized bird?

Such questions have touched a raw nerve in a business that already feels beset by problems. The broiler industry is troubled by what it regards as an unjustified *Salmonella* scare. Egg sales have dropped because of the public's concern over cholesterol. Both industries are caught up in a spiral of ever-expanding production for shrinking profits.

For much of its 4,000-year association with humans the chicken has had an oddly mixed status—part wonder bird, part dumb cluck. On the one hand, in the words of a nursery song, we can eat it both before it's born and after it's dead. On the other hand, it *lets* us—and asks for little more than room to scratch and peck. We don't credit birds with much intelligence, and most of us think of chickens as less than real birds.

It so happens, though, that the chicken's wild forebears—red jungle fowl—still strut and crow in the tropical forests of their native India and Burma. And judging from their behavior, the chicken hasn't changed all that much. Jungle fowl are sociable birds that live in groups with a rigid hierarchy—a pecking order. In spring the cocks fight for territory to share with their hens, then protect them while the hens incubate their eggs and rear their chicks.

Like their domesticated descendants, jungle fowl roosters cry *cock-a-doodle-doo* to herald the sunrise. Humans may have first kept chickens for this symbolic connection with the dawn; in ancient India priests sacrificed chickens to the god of the sun. Other early Asian societies bred the birds for cockfighting. Either way, keeping chickens led in time to surplus eggs and meat. From there it was a short trip to the omelet and the Oven Stuffer.

The jungle fowl adapted easily to domestication. It became a dual-purpose bird—kept for eggs, with meat as a sideline when the bird grew too old to lay. Only early in this century did this sort of barnyard chicken begin to seem inefficient. Modernizing the chicken consisted of two major changes: breeding different types of chicken for meat and for egg production, and moving both operations indoors. Eggs and poultry became two specialized industries.

In the 1950s, in a process called vertical integration, individual companies such as Holly Farms and Perdue began taking over almost all phases of the broiler business, from producing the feed to rearing the chicks to packaging the processed parts. Intense competition forced out small players from the egg industry also. When one researcher told me, "This is a business of a few winners and a lot of losers," he wasn't talking about the chickens.

Almost all commercial chickens are now bred from birds supplied by one of 30 or so breeding companies. Arbor Acres in Glastonbury, Connecticut, supplies 40 percent of the world broiler market. ISA, in Lyon, France, provides birds for two thirds of the international brown-egg industry. Such companies work continuously to improve their breeding lines. The technique is simple: you select birds that are in the top 10 percent for the traits you want, breed them to create a new generation, then take the top 10 percent of that generation, and so on. "We think we can put an additional three to four eggs onto our bird per generation," says Alan Emsley, director of research at ISA Babcock, the French company's U.S. subsidiary.

The breeding companies are in effect genetic countinghouses, where computers keep track of the hundreds of thousands of genetic combinations that can be achieved in controlled matings among the birds. "It's really a mathematical discipline," says Emsley. "We don't tinker with genes in a test tube; the genes we work with are already present in the birds." Getting the right combination of chicken traits, however, is a delicate balancing act. It's possible, for example, to select broilers exclusively for weight gain, but you'll end up with fewer eggs; the two traits tend to be inversely correlated.

For the modern chick, life (and the production line) begins in a commercial hatchery. At a broiler hatchery operated for Holly Farms on the Maryland side of the Delmarva Peninsula, incubators the size of walk-in refrigerators face each other in parallel rows. Each contains about 65,000 eggs in pink trays. The trays are slanted, and every hour they automatically tilt in the opposite direction to duplicate the way a hen turns her eggs in the nest. Most eggs hatch within 21 days.

The chicks, known locally as biddies, are then dumped onto an assembly line. Workers on one side of the line hold the biddies up to a machine that cuts off a third of the upper beak; workers on the opposite side place each chick's neck against an automatic vaccinating machine. The biddies for the most part look dazed; they cheep no more anxiously after their encounter with the machines than they do before. Arguing about how all this affects them, however, is a bit like arguing about how human babies take to circumcision.

(An egg-industry hatchery differs from a broiler hatchery in one important detail: because the egg business requires only hens, the males get "euthanized"—often by being tossed into plastic bags where they suffocate or are crushed to death under their own accumulating weight.)

From the hatchery the chicks get shipped out to farms. These days, however, most farmers simply baby-sit the birds for large companies, following rigid company programs. For broilers and layers alike, high-density indoor housing is the rule. At one typical Delmarva broiler farm a single shed holds 27,000 birds. This shed is only 30 feet wide but almost two football fields long, and the dust kicked up by the chickens forms a haze at either end. The feed comes augering down two 500-foot pipes, automatically keeping the feed stations full. Drinking water, ventilation, and temperatures are likewise automatically controlled.

To keep the birds active and eating, the lights stay on 23 hours a day, with one hour off to accustom them to darkness (a power failure might otherwise cause panic, and darkness is also used to calm the birds before slaughter). This house and the three others on the farm, with a total of more than 100,000 birds, requires only the parttime attention of the farmer, who puts in a full day's work elsewhere as an electrician.

Rearing chickens indoors has advantages other than allowing more birds to be raised in less space with minimal manpower. It also defeats the tyranny of the seasons. In the egg industry, for example, a plant manager can create a permanent artificial springtime by manipulating the amount of daily light the chickens receive. Keeping the birds on a steady 16 hours a day tricks them into thinking that it's the breeding season and stimulates their pituitary glands to release the hormones needed for egg laying. Conversely, the manager can switch off egg production by cutting back on light and feed.

Rearing chickens indoors also allows a company to know exactly what goes into its birds. The company formulates the feed that it ships to its farms. It also routinely samples the feed ingredients, the litter on the chicken house floor, and the slaughtered birds for traces of contaminating pesticides. It even administers medicines when needed, forbidding the farmers to keep poultry pharmaceuticals on the premises.

When the chicken first moved into an artificial environment six decades ago, the losses were often horrendous. By trial and error, by taking away one thing or adding another (vitamin D to replace sunlight, vitamin B_{12} as a substitute for nutrients in meat), researchers learned what chickens needed to live in this new world. Nowadays company computers plan almost every chicken's diet. A "least cost formulation" program considers the nutritional needs of a particular flock (based on such factors as age and seasonal temperature), the nutrients in 30 or so available foods (such as corn, soybean, fish meal, and limestone), and the current cost per nutrient. The computer mulls this over for several seconds, then spits out the combination that fits the bill at the lowest cost.

Precision matters because broiler businesses live or die on the basis of feed-conversion ratio; that is, how many pounds of feed it takes to grow a pound of chicken. The industry standard is two pounds of feed for one pound of chicken. By contrast, it takes six to eight pounds of feed to produce a pound of beef.

Constant pressure to improve this performance has resulted in an astonishing ability to manipulate chicken biology. Dennis Murphy, a poultry extension specialist at the University of Maryland, cites the use of what the industry very delicately terms growth permittants. These are antibiotics used in low doses to alter the bacterial population of the chicken's intestines and improve its uptake of food.

Like other livestock producers, the chicken industry has cut back on the controversial routine use of antibiotics to prevent disease. Critics say that overuse has stimulated antibiotic resistance in bacteria, including bacteria that cause human disease. But the chicken industry still uses antibiotics for certain respira-

tory problems, especially in winter. The law requires a layoff period before slaughter, and the U.S. Department of Agriculture
routinely monitors poultry samples for residues.

Growth permittants are not like other antibiotics, claims Murphy, because they aren't absorbed through the intestines, and
they aren't used in humans. They work by discouraging the
growth of bacteria like staphylococci, streptococci, and clostridia,
which cause scarring and thickening of the intestines even in
healthy birds. Treated chickens have thinner intestinal walls with
more absorptive surface. They grow about 5 percent faster. "It
doesn't sound like much," says Murphy, "but this is a hell of a
margin in your production cost." Rearranging the intestinal bacteria of chickens is also one experimental approach to controlling
salmonellae. A brew of "good bacteria" fed to day-old chicks coats
the intestines and fills up "parking spaces" that might otherwise
be available to harmful bacteria.

Disease control in the modern chicken house is largely a matter of vaccination and isolation. Before entering the Holly Farms
broiler house on Delmarva, visitors put on plastic booties to avoid
introducing disease. Phil Hudspeth, director of research at Holly
Farms, points out that all the birds are the same age: in high-
density housing, it's too risky to mix mature birds with chicks
whose immune systems have not yet developed. On average, 94.5
percent of the birds kept in high-density housing survive to
slaughter, a rate, Murphy says, that no free-range operation can
match.

But the system also has its casualties, according to critics. Some
chicks, they contend, are injured by careless, excessive beak trimming, which leaves the birds unable to feed. Broilers sometimes
suffer such leg weakness that they can't compete for food and risk
being trampled by stronger birds. Both problems have become
animal-welfare issues.

When people in the industry talk about the need for beak
trimming, they tend to blame the chicken's own quarrelsome
nature. Chickens are hierarchical and territorial, which means
that they fight. When an injury draws blood, other birds will peck
at the wound. Cannibalism isn't common, but when it occurs it
can flare up on an epidemic scale. Modern poultry-rearing methods make the problem worse by cramming more birds into less
space (less than a square foot per bird is the broiler-industry
average). To reduce the risk of mayhem, most companies opt for

what they say is the comparatively minor trauma of beak trimming.

Leg weakness is an even trickier problem. Pushing birds to reach market weight at an even earlier age means, in effect, selling overfed babies. In some birds, skeletal development doesn't keep up with weight gain. Moreover, selective breeding has inadvertently turned the broiler into a couch potato. The capacity for rapid weight gain goes hand in hand with the trait of placidity.

But it is the egg industry that draws the most concentrated fire from animal-rights activists, because it compounds high-density housing with caging. The cages tend to be small (commonly 14 by 24 inches), are often crowded (five to seven hens per cage), and may be stacked on top of each other (up to four tiers). The birds stand on slanted cage bottoms, so that their eggs roll out onto a conveyor belt. Another conveyor belt, running just in front of the cage, supplies their feed. One person can thus keep 250,000 laying hens, compared with 3,000 in the old days.

Welfare considerations have already caused Denmark, Switzerland, and the Netherlands to begin modifying or phasing out such battery cages. The European Economic Community has guidelines recommending that each hen have at least 70 square inches of space. In the United States, however, egg-industry groups have so far held out for 48 square inches, the practical minimum.

This is a point of argument even among poultry people. A broiler man I spoke with claimed he could always tell a cage operation simply by the squawking of the birds versus the singsong of the open pen. But when I repeated the remark to Dan Ross, a Connecticut egg producer, he smiled. Standing in the middle of his battery cage operation (with a relatively spacious 60 square inches per bird), he held out his hand to indicate the contented *brek-ek-ek-eking* of the flock.

Even ethologists, people who study animal behavior, admit that it's hard to judge the well-being of caged hens. The moderate point of view, according to Joy Mench of the University of Maryland, is that most production systems prevent chickens from expressing a substantial portion of their natural behavior. "The difficulty," she says, "is determining how important these behaviors are to the bird."

The modern hen, for example, no longer broods—she simply walks away from her eggs. Selective breeding has largely eliminated this trait from laying birds because it interferes with continuous production and egg gathering. But some birds still display "prelaying behavior," pacing frantically for ten minutes before they lay. With five birds to a cage, each producing 250 eggs a year, some birds inevitably get trampled and cut; other birds peck at the wound, and cannibalism may ensue.

Researchers have traced prelaying behavior to two genes, which suggests that careful breeding could weed out the trait. But who can say what function pacing serves in the bird? Who can say how far humans should rearrange chicken behavior to arrive at a chicken that is content in a battery cage?

Another inherent problem with battery cages is that they are filled with what are arguably the birds least suited to caging. Since high egg production correlates with dominant behavior, selective breeding has resulted in more aggressive hens. One way researchers have tried to deal with squabbling chickens is by fitting them with "poly-peepers," special chicken spectacles that limit their vision. (Unfortunately, the spectacles fall off.) But how far should this line of thinking be taken? A 1985 Canadian study found that a blind strain of chicken was not only more docile but more productive, yielding 12.7 percent more eggs. "It is therefore worthwhile," the study's author concluded, "to explore further the potential of this mutation." The logical outcome is to turn the hen into a mechanized, almost inanimate oviduct.

In the present environment, however, what's likely to change is the cage rather than the bird. Poultry scientist Dan Cunningham has studied caged birds for indications of stress. His findings suggest that in the typical high-density cage, birds low in the hierarchy get an inordinate share of the henpecking, have less access to feed, produce fewer eggs, and have enlarged hearts (a sign of long-term stress). But Cunningham has also found that these problems diminish when there are only five birds in the cage, with 60 square inches per bird. He has urged the industry to move toward these standards.

Many egg producers have yet to accept his recommendations. Indeed, many bristle at even the mildest criticisms. (If it weren't for such changes in American agriculture, one poultryman told me, we'd all be scratching in the dirt and speaking Russian.) Meanwhile the Humane Society of the United States has begun an egg boycott, describing the egg as "the breakfast of cruelty." Some groups have gone further: in April of last year a band calling itself the Farm Freedom Fighters raided a Pennsylvania egg operation and painted STOP THE TORTURE on a chicken house. Somewhere down the line, says Cunningham, the two extremes are going to have to find a common ground.

The day I visited Dan Ross at his Connecticut egg farm, I found him working at a metal desk in a packing room partitioned off from one end of a chicken house. He was wearing a red flannel shirt, with a tool kit and a volunteer fire department pager on his belt. Whereas his father raised a few thousand free-range hens, he told me, he now keeps 100,000 in four houses.

"I look at these birds," he said, walking down a row of cages. "They can all lie down. They hardly have to move to get food or water. It's dry, and I try to keep a sixty-degree temperature in winter, with good air quality. When we had an open pen, the litter would get wet and slippery. The chickens walked around in their own filth. We had roundworm and other diseases transmitted through droppings."

It might be possible to improve on the caging system, Ross supposed, but the whole industry would have to change (for that matter, the whole world, since American eggs compete in the international market). It isn't something an individual farmer can afford to do. He pulled out a report for 1986, a good year, showing that it cost him 44.59 cents to produce a dozen eggs, which sold for 45.4 cents. In 1987, he said, he lost money on every egg. He was worried about competition from Rose Acres, an egg ranch in Indiana with 12 million hens. While Ross has to have four pound of feed shipped from the Midwest to produce a dozen eggs, Rose Acres, in the middle of the Corn Belt, simply ships the dozen eggs.

Ross tried to imagine what it must be like to run a business of that size. "A guy with twelve million chickens doesn't have much time to enjoy his chickens," Ross said. "A guy with twelve million chickens has a lot of other things on his mind." He paused for a moment and reflected. "But that's the history of the business in this country. You just get bigger and bigger."

THE AMERICAN HUNTER UNDER FIRE[3]

Bruce Wargo hoped to bag a brace of pheasant or grouse, perhaps a few cottontails during a hunting trip last October to Connecticut's Paugussett State Forest. What he got instead was a rude surprise. A covey of animal-rights activists flushed *him* from the brush. They dogged his every move, hectored him about the evils of hunting and promised to annoy him until he left the woods. When Wargo, 43, an auto-body-repairshop owner from Monroe, Conn., raised his 20-gauge shotgun to shift its balance for carrying comfort, one blocked the muzzle with his bare hand and begged him not to shoot. "I said to the guy: 'Are you nuts?'" the hunter recalls. "If this kind of stuff goes on, somebody's gonna get accidentally killed."

Increasingly, the cacophony of air horns, loud music and angry shouting augments, the crack of rifles and the blast of shotguns in the nation's fields, forests and wetlands as protesters attempt to block or disrupt hunts. After successfully turning the once obscure issues of laboratory animals and fur wearing into full-fledged national debates, animal activists now scent a new quarry. Several national organizations are spearheading the anti-hunting campaign and have scored early hits in courts and in state legislatures to block hunts. "We want to stigmatize hunting, we see it as the next logical target and we believe it is vulnerable," says Wayne Pacelle, national director of the Fund for Animals and organizer of the Paugussett protest.

Three broad questions dominate the debate. Is it moral and ethical for sentient creatures to be killed for sport or trophies? With many species dwindling due to environmental pressures, does hunting threaten to tip the balance against America's wildlife populations? Are hunters friends or foes of the environmental movement? If hunters cannot convince their potential adversaries in the conservation movement that they are anxious to preserve America's wild species, they will face a far greater challenge to their recreation than the one posed by animal-rights advocates.

This attack on the nation's Nimrods is one of several developments that portend major changes for hunters. Nearly 16 million

[3]Reprint of an article by Michael Satchell. *U.S. News & World Report*. 108:30-1+.
F 5 '90. Copyright 1990 by U.S. News & World Report, Inc. All rights reserved.

Americans—7 percent of the population—bought hunting licenses last year to pursue what for some is a pastime, for others a passion. The burgeoning political battle to make hunters an endangered species comes at a time when America's wildlife is under mounting assault from other fronts. Urbanization and the resulting loss of wildlife habitat, particularly in riparian and wetland areas, along with rampant poaching for trophy animals and commercial gain are squeezing vulnerable populations from waterfowl to big game. Joel Scrafford, a senior agent with the U.S. Fish and Wildlife Service in Montana, believes that "at some point in the future, the public will look back and realize this was a pivotal juncture for saving our wild animals."

Shoot-anything Rambos

Even in places where game is plentiful, hunting restrictions are mounting. Farmers, fed up with so-called slob hunters, are increasingly denying permission to stalk their acreage or are charging hefty fees for the privilege. "We're seeing fewer skilled hunters who can cut a track and follow it all day." Scrafford laments. "Now, we see too many four-wheel-drive, assault-rifle, gun-and-run, shoot-anything yahoos who think they're Rambo."

Shrinking opportunities for good hunting on public land are promoting a steady rise in private game preserves where the challenge is minimal, fees are high, targets are often preselected and the kill is assured. Most dedicated game stalkers like Steve Judd, a student at Virginia's Radford University, say they relish the companionship, field craft and traditions of hunting more than the kill. "I don't care if I get a deer and neither do my friends," Judd says. "Being outside, tramping the hedgerows on a crisp morning, that's as important as shooting something. Killing is only a tiny part of the overall experience." Like others, the crew-cut economics major worries that in the distant future, hunting could evolve into a European-style activity where only the wealthy can afford to shoot on private reservations.

Not surprisingly, the ranks of hunters have dwindled by 700,000 since 1975. In an aging population, strenuous activities like hunting tend to lose their appeal. As people move from the countryside to the cities, convenient shooting opportunities shrink and other diversions beckon. The rise in single-parent homes means sons raised by mothers are far less likely to be initiated into blood sports. In some states, the hunting population has crashed like a herd of starving deer. California, which in 1970 had 750,000 licensed hunters, was down to 415,000 last year. Florida, with its relentless influx of urban retirees, is considered a ripe anti-hunting target. A referendum would most likely ban hunting there, fears National Rifle Association (NRA) Assistant Director of Hunter Services Dennis Eggers.

In the harvest-or-holocaust debate, hunters, with their vested interest in maintaining a healthy supply of prey, regard themselves as front-line conservationists. Since President Theodore Roosevelt, an avid hunter, founded the federal wildlife refuge system in 1903, hunters have invested their dollars and energies to preserve habitat and restore game populations depleted by development, disease, pollution and indiscriminate overkill.

Without hunting, enthusiasts argue, game species would decrease in public value and the will to preserve them would erode. Hunters also point out that nonhunting wildlife lovers—who pay no license fees or excise taxes—can photograph or view deer, waterfowl, upland birds and other game species year-round. Hunting advocates note they are the prime revenue source for preserving nonendangered wildlife. Last year, they paid $517 million for licenses, duck stamps and excise taxes on equipment and ammunition, much of it used to finance game-research-and-management programs and to help purchase habitat that benefits all creatures. Wyoming rancher, outfitter and professional conservationist John Turner, who currently heads the U.S. Fish and Wildlife Service, deplores the efforts to end hunting. "If you eliminate this constituency, you lose the greatest source of conservation revenue," Turner says. "You also do away with a vital cultural and historical aspect of American life."

This legacy harkens back at least 150 years, when the nation teemed with wildlife. Sixty million bison, 100,000 grizzly bears, 50,000 bald eagles and uncounted herds of elk, antelope and bighorn sheep inhabited the frontier. Passing flocks of passenger pigeons darkened the sky for 2 to 3 hours at a time, and varmint shooters could plink away in prairie-dog towns 25 miles in diameter. The nation's woodlands, rangelands, and wetlands were alive with mountain lions, bobcats, wolves, black bears, beavers, otters, minks and waterfowl. It was a hunter's paradise. And it was almost lost.

Greedy and indiscriminate killing for meat, fur, feathers and sport in the latter half of the 19th century pushed several of these

species close to extinction, and the last passenger pigeon died in
1914 in the Cincinnati Zoo. This slaughter prompted new hunting laws and the rise of the modern conservation movement,
which brought many of these populations back from the brink.
Today, some heavily managed game species like white-tailed deer,
pheasant and quail have become plentiful, but observers on both
sides of the gunsight believe much of the nation's wildlife is approaching a critical time.

Animal-rights activists argue that silencing the guns will help
such regionally hard-pressed species as black bear, antelope,
mountain lion and bighorn sheep. A hunting ban would also
bring respite for the nation's ducks—an environmental-barome-
ter species that has been decimated by the loss of wetlands in its
northern breeding and southern wintering areas. Despite increasingly restrictive seasons and bag limits, last autumn's flight
was down to 64 million birds, slightly above 1985's record low of
62 million. From 1969 through 1979, annual flights averaged
91.5 million before the decline began. Another ominous indica-
tor: Breeding populations of 9 of the 10 key duck species were
also down last year. Only canvasbacks increased in number, by a
modest 12 percent.

While most mainstream conservation organizations tacitly
support tightly controlled hunting, some are beginning to challenge the hunter-dominated state fish and game agencies. The
conservationists want the agencies to end their concentration on
enhancing game populations and devote more attention to other
wildlife. Last week, the Animal Legal Defense Fund sued to challenge the Massachusetts Fisheries and Wildlife Board, which requires a majority of the seven-member commission to be licensed
hunters or trappers. "Having hunters oversee wildlife," says
Pacelle of the Fund for Animals, "is like having Dracula guard the
blood bank."

Pacelle argues that ending such widespread practices as clear-
ing brushland, damming streams and killing predators to boost
deer, waterfowl and upland game birds will mean more habitat
for everything from songbirds to varmints. More important, it
will restore a more naturally balanced ecosystem. "No wildlife
resource agency in the country has a coherent systematic approach to preserve habitat and prevent massive extinctions of
plant and animal life," believes Sara Vickerman, regional director
of Defenders of Wildlife in the Pacific Northwest.

Rising Public Opposition

It is that emerging challenge from mainstream environmentalists that could be most devastating to hunters over time as growing numbers of Americans are attracted to the ecology movement. Moreover, there seems to be a latent sentiment against hunters that might be tapped by their opponents. Hunting for meat or sport has been a critical element in America's self-reliant pioneer tradition, but today's attitudes depend largely on how and why animals are killed. Studies by Yale Prof. Stephen Kellert indicate steadily rising public opposition. While more than 80 percent of Americans approve of hunting to put game on the table—be it a native Alaskan subsistence hunter or a white-collar suburbanite with a taste for low-cholesterol venison—80 percent also feel hunting for trophy heads to mount on the wall is wrong. Some 60 percent disapprove of hunting merely for sport or recreation. About 1 in 3 Americans, according to Kellert's studies, favors a total ban.

Building on this sentiment is the goal of the anti-hunting forces, who launched their campaign in earnest about a decade ago. Demonstrations in the field have become so widespread that powerful hunting lobbies in 35 states have persuaded lawmakers to make it illegal to harass hunters. Most other states have similar laws pending, and there is a corresponding bill with more than 50 cosponsors in Congress. Some 30 states also make it a crime to haze animals for their protection during hunting season. This projects an improbable scenario where it is legal to put a bullet into a deer but unlawful to scream at it: "Vamoose! You're gonna get shot!"

However, anti-hunting forces have scored some important court victories. In the first definitive constitutional test of harassment laws, Connecticut's law was determined not to be a compelling state interest and was voided by a U.S. appeals court. That's why game wardens stood by and watched as protesters hounded Bruce Wargo from Paugussett State Park last October. Another legal challenge is now before the courts in Maryland, where the harassment law is regarded as the national model. If it is struck down, anti-hunters are confident they'll benefit from a domino effect.

In California, opponents have blocked mountain-lion and bear hunts by convincing judges that state wildlife biologists have no accurate count of these dwindling big-game populations. Next

June, Californians will vote on a ballot initiative that will be closely watched by the hunting fraternity. The measure would ban mountain-lion hunting except where human life or livestock is threatened [the bill was passed]. Activists have also stymied bear hunting in New Jersey, blocked plans to initiate dove hunting in Michigan, Ohio and New York and halted expansion of hunting in Texas state parks.

The activists' strategy also relies on the emotional issue of cruelty. Last autumn, a number of demonstrations were targeted at bowhunting for deer, which protesters hate because so many animals are crippled by arrows and wander off to suffer lingering deaths. Studies in Texas over 15 years show that only half the deer hit by bowhunters are retrieved, compared with 90 percent for gunners.

Anti-hunting forces reaped a public-relations bonanza last winter, when 569 bison lumbered over the northern boundary of Yellowstone National Park in search of food. Each was shot by a lottery-winning hunter at virtual pointblank range. Justification for the slaughter was that the bison posed a threat—albeit remote—of transmitting brucellosis to Montana cattle. Published accounts and gory videotape of exultant hunters gunning down hundreds of the nation's most enduring historical wildlife icons enraged many Americans and resulted in an emergency U.S. congressional hearing. For many serious hunters priding themselves on outdoor skills and marksmanship, the spectacle of the bison-shooting gallery was disturbing. "It resulted in bad press," agrees the NRA's Eggers. "People in big cities didn't like it, and I understand their feelings."

Seeking Common Ground

Largely lost as the hunting-morality debate intensifies is the fact that many proponents on both sides of the issue share the same basic goal: Preserving the vitality of these treasured species. Front-line observers like U.S. Fish and Wildlife chief Turner believe there is enough common ground between hunters and the nation's 135 million nonhunting wildlife enthusiasts that some kind of reconciliation oriented toward environmental issues ought to be possible. "The real tragedy [for wildlife] is pollution, pesticides, urbanization, deforestation, hazardous waste, lack of water and wetland destruction," Turner says. "I get tears in my eyes when I see this self-destructive waste of energy by the anti-

hunting groups. Let's focus our main energies on mutual interests
and arm-wrestle on the other."

One hopeful sign for those like Turner who hope for a nar-
rowing of differences is the revulsion hunters and nonhunters
alike feel for the dramatic rise in commercial poaching and unlawful trophy hunting that reached record levels in the Rocky
Mountain West last year. Asian demand for gallbladders of bear
and antlers of elk and antelope, both regarded in the Orient as
having valuable medicinal properties, is exerting tremendous
pressure on these animals.

Illegal hunters face little threat of arrest from the thinly
spread force of 5,200 federal and state wildlife enforcement officers. World-class elk, moose, deer, mountain goats and bighorn
sheep protected year-round in Yellowstone, Glacier, Denali,
Olympic and other crown-jewel national parks are now being
killed by trophy hunters brazenly invading these once sacrosanct
preserves. Habitat destruction, the single biggest threat to wildlife, also makes life easier for poachers by squeezing game into
smaller areas, thus making them more vulnerable. And poaching's negative effect is twofold. While commercial hunting often
ravages local populations, the frantic competition for record-
book trophies has perhaps a more insidious effect by robbing the
gene pool of the biggest, healthiest and best of the species. "More
and more people are competing for trophies out of fear that
they'd better get them now or there won't be any left," says 25-
year veteran enforcement agent Joel Scrafford. He notes that
wealthy collectors will pay unscrupulous guides up to $5,000 to
shoot a grizzly and $45,000 to kill the four native species of North
American sheep—hunting's so-called grand slam.

Federal sting operations have smashed several organized
poaching rings, and conservation organizations have joined the
fight. A public appeal for contributions by the Izaak Walton
League of America, a conservation and pro-hunting organization, raised $600,000 to purchase a helicopter and two airboats
for use by agents in their antipoaching efforts. The National
Parks and Conservation Association has set up a national toll-free
hot line—(800) 448-NPCA—to report poaching in the national
parks.

Outside this realm, though, it is still an open question whether
hunters and their foes will seek common ground or confrontation. On their choice may depend the future well-being of America's ever precarious, increasingly threatened wildlife heritage.

ALL HEAVEN IN A RAGE[4]

In 1663, Robert Hooke took a conscious dog, cut away its ribs and diaphragm, severed its trachea so that the nose of a bellows could be inserted, and blew air into the lungs to keep the animal alive, thus proving that the motion of the lungs was not essential to respiration. With its windpipe cut, the animal could not give voice to its suffering, but Hooke was acutely aware of its distress. He wrote to Robert Boyle:

I shall hardly be induced to make any further trials of this kind, because of the torture of the creature: but certainly the enquiry would be very noble, if we could any way find a way so as to stupify the creature, as that it might not be sensible, which I fear there is hardly any opiate will perform.

Nonetheless, Hooke did conduct the experiment once more, in 1667, before the Fellows of the Royal Society.

This famous episode from the early history of animal experimentation in Britain raises many of the issues which were to dominate its subsequent development. In the first place, it suggests how anaesthetic techniques, when they finally came to be applied in the mid-nineteenth century, were to have a dual consequence. They could render animals insensible to procedures which previously had caused great pain, but in so doing they were also to enlarge immeasurably the possibilities of such experimentation. More importantly, Hooke's experiment gave rise to the contradictory responses on which an entire ethical and scientific controversy has been built.

The Fellows of the Royal Society were almost unanimously impressed, not by Hooke's conclusion (which Vesalius, after all, had noted a century and a half earlier) but by the fact that it could be demonstrated empirically. This explains their requests to see it performed again and again, and Sprat, in his contemporary *History of the Royal Society* tells us that others were appointed to re-enact the procedure when Hooke refused. Of the observers, only John Evelyn seems to have shared Hooke's misgivings, commenting in his diary that 'this was an experiment of more cruelty than pleased me.' Nonetheless, it was continually performed until the

[4]Article by historian Macdonald Daly. *History Today.* 37:7-9. My '87. Copyright 1987 by History Today Ltd.

late eighteenth century, when Stephen Hales and John Hunter
devised identical or near-identical procedures.

An alternative critical reaction was caricature of the type employed by Swift. In *Gulliver's Travels* (1726), Hooke is ridiculed as
the deranged Physician at the Academy of Lagado, who blows up
a dog by inserting a bellows into its anus and then attempts to
resuscitate the dead animal by the same operation. This tells us
more about Swift's particular animus towards Hooke than any
general concern for animals, but his moral disapproval in this
particular case is clear.

Anti-vivisectionists have always been ready to associate great
cultural figures with their cause, on the assumption that their
finer feelings lend them moral authority. Thus Johnson and Pope
have been hailed as the progenitors of the modern movement for
humane science, and there is some basis for the claim. Johnson
did explicitly denounce a great deal of the scientific work of his
day which involved the infliction of suffering on animals as the
activity of 'a race of wretches' and called for 'universal resentment' against it. Yet he could further the career of one of its
proponents, his physician and good friend William Cruikshank,
whom he even remembered in his will. Pope, similarly, could
condemn the 'barbarities' of Stephen Hales and, in the same
breath, call him a 'good man.'

It would be more accurate to view the two centuries after
Hooke as the pre-history both of vivisection and its opposition.
Published reports in the *Philosophical Transactions of the Royal Society* show, as one might expect, an admixture of serious and trivial
experimental ventures, but do not give a reliable general picture.
With no legal or statistical monitoring of the practice before the
advent of the 1876 Cruelty to Animals Act (under which 270
experiments on living vertebrates were licensed in 1878), it is
impossible to take an informed overview of the scope of experimentation in this period.

What one can say with confidence is that the challenge to
vivisection grew tremendously within much broader social and
political developments. Chartism established in Britain an un-
precedentedly combative approach to social reform. If it is unlikely that the nature and extent of animal experimentation
changed markedly between Charles II and Victoria, dissent
against it had become mobilised and organised in a manner previously unimaginable. The combination of petitioning and pressure groupings—there is evidence that anti-vivisection societies

existed as early as the 1860s—is an obvious Chartist legacy. But the social composition of the early anti-vivisection movement proper was of professional and leisured middled class, with a sprinkling from the aristocracy. In fact, had it not been for constitutional reasons, the movement would have included Queen Victoria herself, who wrote to Gladstone in April 1881:

With pleasure that Mr Gladstone takes an interest in that dreadful subject of vivisection, in which she has done all she could, and she earnestly hopes that Mr Gladstone will take an opportunity of speaking strongly against a practice which is a disgrace to humanity and Christianity.

A great deal of ink has been spilled in attempting to understand how this relatively marginal Victorian social problem provoked such a furore. Even in 1885 there were less than 800 animals used in Britain for this purpose. If that were the present number, it is difficult to believe that the protests of modern anti-vivisection societies would be taken seriously (the present annual figure, in fact, is three and a quarter million). No doubt the humanitarians had a sense (well-grounded, as the subsequent history reveals), that if vivisection went unchecked at this juncture it was likely to become a major scientific method, and there were additional fears that if it remained acceptable to use animals it would be no large step to start experimenting on humans. But the crucial factor in their success is that they were organised at the very centre of the establishment. There were literary figures aplenty in their number. Tennyson, Browning, Lewis Carroll and Carlyle all lent their support, just as Shaw, Galsworthy, Hardy and John Cowper Powys were to do in the next century. Ruskin even went to the length of resigning his professorship at Oxford when a laboratory for vivisection was established there in 1885. Lord Shaftesbury, Cardinal Manning and the Archbishop of York were all involved in the Victoria Street Society (now the National Anti-Vivisection Society), established largely by Frances Cobbe in 1876.

A year earlier, the introduction by Lord Henniker of a *Bill for Regulating the Practice of Vivisection* had led the Government to issue a Royal Commission of Enquiry into the matter. Its report led to a new Bill prohibiting the use of cats, horses and dogs and requiring the use of anaesthesia in all other species, but the Cruelty to Animals Act which finally emerged in August 1876 enforced none of these measures. Technically, it made anaesthesia mandatory, but in practice exemption certificates were easily obtained. Protests that the licensing and inspection provisions offered no

protection to the animals but, on the contrary, sheltered researchers from publicity and prosecution seem, in retrospect, to
have been justified: in its 110-year history there were no prosecu-
tions under the Act.

Shaftesbury was right to point out that, however inadequate,
the Act was a major advance. The first of its kind in the world, it
provided a foundation to which amendments could be made. But
he would not have been so optimistic had he envisaged over a
century of legislative inaction. Some of the responsibility for this
failure must be laid at the door of the anti-vivisectionists themselves. Their movement became almost immediately fragmented.
Her hopes frustrated, Cobbe left the Victoria Street Society to
found the British Union for the Abolition of Vivisection, which
pressed in vain for an immediate end to experimentation by a
single legislative act. While the humanitarians squabbled over tactics, animal experimentation consolidated its position in the biological sciences.

The annual returns to the Home Secretary in 1910 showed
that over 95,000 living animals had been used in scientific experiments likely to cause pain. But events in the Edwardian period
indicate that vivisection could unite as well as divide social groups
which were normally at odds. Coral Lansbury (in her *The Old
Brown Dog: Women, Workers and Vivisection in Edwardian England*)
has recently explored the peculiar co-operation between London
feminists and trade unionists in defending the symbolic statue of
an experimental terrier dog from medical students attempting to
destroy it. The statue was erected in Battersea Park in 1906 by the
International Anti-Vivisection Council, and a year later provoked
students of London's University College (where the dog had been
killed) to disturbances, demonstrations and a full-scale riot with
local citizens. The statue was removed in 1910 because the cost of
protecting it had become exorbitant.

Trade unionists were usually antagonistic towards feminists
because women were paid at a lower rate and could thus oust men
from jobs, but in this instance both groups seem to have shared a
deep distrust of the orthodox medical profession. The image of a
conscious dog powerless on the operating table was all too remi-
niscent of the forced feeding of imprisoned suffragettes, and
both were a consequence of institutional domination by men.
Poorly-paid manual workers generally experienced dreadful
treatment from doctors in modern hospitals, which they associated, rightly or wrongly, with the violence those same doctors

often inflicted on animals. They preferred to attend the 'anti-vivisection' hospitals (where animal work was forbidden) and undertook tremendous fundraising ventures when the finances of these institutions were squeezed.

The Great War [1914–1918] put an end to the anti-vivisection movement for half a century and more. This was an unseasonable decline, as the real boom in animal experimentation occurred in the inter-war period. The rise reflects the multiplication of fields in which animal experiments have come to form a part. In 1939 the annual number of animals used was approaching a million and enlarging steadily. By 1960 it was over 3½ million and in 1970 over 5½ million.

It is difficult to place precisely the remarkable resurrection of the anti-vivisection movement in recent times. Certainly pressure was intense enough by 1983 for the Conservative Government to feel the need to suggest a substitute for the Cruelty to Animals Act. The proposals were strongly challenged as inadequate by the main anti-vivisection societies, and the scientific establishment welcomed them. As the Animals (Scientific Procedures) Act has been in force only since January of this year, it is too early to judge its effects. Symbolically enough, the Brown Dog was replaced on its pedestal in Battersea Park in 1985. But curiously (or perhaps *not* curiously) there have been no attempts as yet to remove it.

FUZZY-WUZZY THINKING ABOUT ANIMAL RIGHTS[5]

Early last year on a business trip to the eastern Sierras, I stopped for dinner at an upscale ski-country restaurant. At a table to my left a man was expounding to his wife. "Hitler had a good idea," he began, the sort of conversational opener that commands instant attention. "Not killing Jews," he said, and as everyone within earshot exhaled he added, "but killing lowlife scum." I strained to overhear a precise definition, but his wife had apparently issued a nonverbal death threat if he did not lower his voice. In the ensuing hush I picked up another conversation, from a

[5]Reprinted by permission of author Richard Conniff. From *Audubon*. 92:121+. N '90. Copyright 1990 by the National Audubon Society.

table to my right, about war games. "There's a certain pleasure in shooting someone," a nouveau California man was remarking, quite genially.

I slid down on my banquette, out of the line of fire, and buried my face in page 12A of the *Reno Gazette-Journal,* where my eyes came to rest in myopic proximity to two headlines:

Private Library Disinherited
for Evicting Muffin the Cat
and
Medical Research Group Sets Up
Pension Plan for Ailing Chimps

Every life has its little epiphanies, and this was one of mine. As I hovered over my newspaper (the private library was out $30,000; the pension plan was going to divert $1.8 million from AIDS research) and eavesdropped on the genocideal fantasies of my fellow diners, what dawned on me was how thoroughly the modern world has accepted the worthlessness of human beings and, in equal and opposite measure, the sentimental importance of individual animal lives.

I suppressed the urge to protest, in part because it seemed somehow out of character. Like George Bush and just about everybody else in this great consumer society of ours, I think of myself as an environmentalist for whom animals are important— as populations, if not as individuals. Human overabundance being the main threat to the natural world, it follows without much difficulty that I am also a misanthrope, perhaps more explicitly than most environmentalists (having once published a book with the dedication, "To hell with you all"). And yet I couldn't suppress the thought that our scheme of shared values was going topsy-turvily askew, and that misanthropy, which was all very well as an aberration, was beginning to be a dangerously commonplace self-indulgence. Like a bad marriage, society was degenerating into a foul entanglement characterized by mutual loathing and moral one-upmanship, wherein the milk of human kindness flowed only for Muffin the cat.

This same feeling came back to me over and over last winter, as animal rights activists captured the public imagination with their anti-fur campaign. Americans suddenly seemed to be painfully conscious that every human action has a consequence for other life-forms; they were beginning to weigh costs for the natural world against supposed benefits for people, without so much of the usual bias. A worthy development, which environmentalists might normally be expected to hail. Unfortunately, the tendency in formulating such equations is to start with issues that have no effect whatsoever on one's own way of life, and to a lot of people, fur sounded like just the thing.

The clash of the titans took place in Wonderland—Aspen, Colorado—where fistfights broke out in fern bars and friend-ships ended in stony silence over a proposed ban on the sale of furs. Advocates of the ban argued that no animal should have to suffer to produce something as frivolous as a fur coat. The indus-try replied that a ban on fur was merely a preamble to the animal liberation movement's broader agenda of ending "all animal ex-ploitation." "Today fur," said one industry advertisement. "To-morrow leather. Then wool. Then meat." Aspen voters, who re-buked the trade by banning the leghold trap in 1986, apparently decided that they did not also need to risk offending rich tourists and defeated the new measure by a margin of almost two-to-one.

Ordinary Americans otherwise confronted the fur issue vicariously through their favorite entertainment celebrities, with noted deep thinker and bathing-suit-competition host Bob Bar-ker providing a philosophical lead. Candice Bergen, lending her support to The Humane Society, declared that she would wear fur only "to make the statement that a character is dim-wit-ted . . . self-absorbed . . . and unenlightened." As if to personify this new Hollywood orthodoxy, Suzanne Sugarbaker wore a fur on an episode of *Designing Women*, and did one really need to say more?

One did. Suzy "Chapstick" Chaffee, who has her own fur fash-ion line, managed to be both cold-blooded and starry-eyed in defense of the trade: "I wish the animal rights extremists would give their fur coats to the homeless," she told *New York* magazine, sounding as if she were working from a Sugarbaker script. "The fur industry does it every year at Grand Central station, and it's one of the most inspiring things I've ever done." Chaffee pointed out correctly that animals in the wild seldom make it to the old-folks home. They suffer cruel deaths from starvation and disease. The fur trade was really just a form of "tough love," she declared, doubtless causing parents of teenagers everywhere to wonder if what they really needed was a nice leghold trap.

Despite winning the vote, and even despite Suzy Chaffee, the fur industry made no new friends among the general public. Animal activists scored all the emotional points. They had better visuals: a photo of a gnawed-off paw in a leghold trap and a television commercial of fur-clad models sweeping down a run-way, spattering the audience with blood. They had better slogans: "Get a feel for fur: Slam your fingers in a car door." They had rock stars seeking the limelight who were certain as *People* put it, that they'd "tapped into the next big social issue." They were winning the public relations war by appealing not merely to human empathy for brown-eyed animals, but also to normal human resentment against rich people. At a demonstration in New York, I saw an older woman with knots of terminal dissatis-faction at the corners of her mouth carrying a sign: "Ms. Macho woman wears her cruel status trophy to the office. Never under-estimate her haughty inhumanity." To animals, I wondered, or to secretaries?

The anti-fur movement was winning, above all, because it was so easy. You want to save the animals? Stop wearing fur. Hell, most of us never wore fur in the first place. Better yet, for those inclined to moral fascism, you could pin a "Fur Is Murder" button onto the strap of your leather shoulder bag and glare cigarette-smoking, fur-clad lowlife scum back into the Stone Age where they belonged. Or wait till one of them settled down beside you on the bus, then shriek, "Get that dead animal away from me!" Talk about empowerment!

By now you have probably discerned that I had a few philo-sophical and tactical problems with the animal rights movement, beginning with the daunting realization that these people were a lot like me. I grew up in a comfortable New Jersey suburb where what we meant by wildlife was principally the gray squirrel, and the only known trap was a Havahart. This is, I'm sure, the way most adult Americans have grown up: in towns that blend into one another with no open space in between, dependent on the remote and unimaginable three percent of the population who do the agricultural work to feed and clothe the rest of us.

Until I shopped for food in other countries, where carcasses hung in shop windows and butchers sawed off ribs while I waited, it never occurred to me how divorced I'd become from the deaths of even our domestic animals. I have eaten bacon (a.k.a. hog belly) all my life, but distinctly remember the first time I saw it on the hoof. It was at a gas station on Interstate 80 in Iowa, and when another customer said he needed water for his hog, I thought he was talking about a motorcycle. I was twenty years old.

What this kind of upbringing means is that people like me have been able to live all our lives under the illusion that nature is essentially benign, and that death is the exception rather than the daily rule. We long not for protection from nature, but for some fleeting sense of oneness with it. We believe, as one animal rights pamphlet puts it, "that the various species of sentient creatures on Earth constitute a single, complex, interconnected, and mutually dependent web of life, and that humans are part of, not apart from, this biological network." One could hardly ask for a more satisfactory statement of environmentalism, except perhaps to delete the word "sentient" so as not to exclude insects and even bacteria, on which the web of life is no less dependent.

But what this sort of suburban pantheism lacked for me was any sense of the first law of nature, which I knew at least by reputation: Eat or be eaten. Or more precisely: Eat and be eaten. "Blessed are the animals," the congregation at a recent New York memorial service for animals solemnly intoned, "for they shall lead us back to our lost innocence . . . Blessed are all wild, free things, for they live in harmony with their mother." In this world view, animals apparently laid down their heads and died in their sleep to a crescendo of violins, and the corpses were wafted on pillowy clouds to Valhalla.

I picked up a brochure from the sponsoring organization, Trans-Species Unlimited (TSU). On the cover was a picture of a woman and a polar bear gazing at each other across a barrier. The woman appeared to be contemplating the bear's soulful eyes and huggable demeanor. The caption, arguably ill-considered, said, "REACH OUT." I don't pretend to know what the bear was contemplating, but in my exurban adult life I have had the opportunity to examine an elk calf that had recently come within reach of a bear and two cubs. Roughly 90 percent of its biomass had achieved a kind of oneness with nature. The bears had been particularly assiduous about cracking open the brain pan like a coconut, licking out the contents, and reducing the skull to a few indigestible splinters. Flies were already working to exploit the remaining grease spots as a future home for maggots.

I mention these unseemly details to suggest that if people wished to think clearly about nature, the proper context was not Muffin the cat but an eviscerated elk calf. Nature is a slaughterhouse—vast, brutal, gory, and efficient. If we were to follow its example, we would kill whatever we wanted, whenever we want-

ed, by whatever means came in handy. Happily, we do not do so.
Though they sometimes prove inadequate, we have laws to protect animals from needless human cruelty and overharvesting.

But the core of the suburban pantheist, animal rights, anti-fur
movement was that such laws could never be enough, no matter
how strict. Over and over, groups like TSU and People for the
Ethical Treatment of Animals (PETA) stated that the real issue
wasn't whether the animal was killed cruelly or for a mere status
symbol. Asked about the use of leather, which was inexplicably
gaining status at the same time fur was becoming a social stigma, a
PETA spokesman said, "That's the next step . . . it was easier to
start with fur." Their essential argument was that humans have no
right to kill any sentient creature, for any reason. What the animal rights movement seems to be urging was that we separate
ourselves from any direct dependence on animals, pull back into
our suburbs, and withdraw from nature. And people were buying
it, out of moral exhaustion with the vast challenge of minimizing
environmental consequences in more meaningful ways.

At the memorial service in New York, a woman dressed in
mourning stood before a coffin heaped with discarded fur coats.
With a rosy glow of righteousness about the cheekbones, she
raised her fist and declared, "This struggle will not end until
every creature on Earth is free." I had read that some animal
liberationists objected to the use of silk as a grotesque exploitation
of silkworms, and to honey as theft from honeybees. I wondered
if making every creature on Earth free meant that the speaker
intended to restrain the copper-colored fly known as *Bufolucilia
silvarum,* which deposits its eggs in the nostrils of toads and frogs.
When the larvae hatch, they blind their hosts and devour them.
In the interest of preventing needless slaughter, would she speak
sternly to the great horned owl, which may decapitate fifteen
adult common terns but eat just one? Would she admonish the
mink, which is capable of wiping out whole muskrat families in a
senseless killing frenzy? Would she issue sound dietary edicts to
the bulimic Adélie penguin, which sometimes causes itself to
vomit, the better to kill and consume more fish?

These everyday animal transgressions against common decen-
cy did not come to mind with the idea that they might somehow
justify human depredations. What I was getting at was an apparent contradiction in the animal rights philosophy. How could animal liberationists argue on the one hand that humans were mere-

ly a part of nature, no better or worse than other animals, and on the other that our species alone was obliged to give up practices with which it has naturally evolved, like killing and eating animals and wearing their skins? How could they argue that humans have no inherent moral superiority, and at the same time argue that we have a high moral obligation to treat animals more humanely than they would treat us or each other?

A minister took the microphone and began to suggest a parallel between animal liberation and black liberation. He recounted his recent decision to picket that squalid bastion of animal enslavement and whip-cracking Simon Legrees, the circus, and drawing himself up with as much fervor as a Unitarian can manage, declared, "Like Malcolm X, I do not condone violence. But by whatever means necessary, we will defend ourselves."

The new sin of our day, as vile as racism and sexism, was speciesism, the attitude that humans have a right to exploit other species. In the new animal rights orthodoxy, the needs of a laboratory mouse deserved equal consideration with the needs of a sick child. "I don't believe human beings have the 'right to life.' That's a supremacist perversion. A rat is a pig is a dog is a boy," PETA co-director Ingrid Newkirk once declared, giving the idea its most concise Orwellian formulation. The suffering of animals was morally equivalent to the suffering of humans: "Six million Jews died in concentration camps," Newkirk also declared on another occasion, "but six billion broiler chickens will die this year in slaughterhouses." (Holocaust and slavery analogies are by their nature garish and demeaning to the victims, but this example surely pushes the form to its imaginable limits.)

The trouble with speciesism as a cause for indignation was that it seemed to be just about universal in the animal kingdom. By definition, a species is a group of physically and genetically similar individuals which interbreed and also often cooperate, the better to eat other species and forestall the time of being eaten. What the pejorative emphasis on speciesism suggests to me is a sense of human worthlessness, or more specifically, the worthlessness of other people.

Human self-loathing has of course been around for some time now. Among environmentalists sharing two or three beers, for example, the notion is quite common that if only some calamity could wipe out the entire human race, other species might once again have a chance. The trouble with this noble and self-sacrificing stance is that it almost always winds up being compromised so that some select group of *other* people gets wiped out. One can hear hints of this in the Earth First! approach to AIDS as "a welcome development in the inevitable reduction of human population." (Defying logical consistency, leaders of the movement have not yet announced the addition of unsafe sex to tree spiking on their personal agendas.) One can hear it much more clearly in the remarks of Ingrid Newkirk, who must not realize that in likening chicken slaughterhouses to death camps she echoes something Heinrich Himmler once said: "We Germans, who are the only people in the world who have a decent attitude toward animals, will also assume a decent attitude toward these human animals." It should not need saying this late in the game, but devaluing human life and deifying animals is a dangerous solution.

It is also irrational. Though it grieves me as a misanthrope to say so, humanity remains the most noble creation of this planet (and the more firmly we keep this idea in mind, the more nobly, or the less deplorably, we tend to behave). If we want to argue that humans have a moral obligation to treat animals decently, as we surely do, we must also acknowledge that the obligation exists because humans possess a highly evolved moral sensibility—a sensibility that is so unlike anything in the animal world as to call forth the forbidden word "superior." (Animal rights activists condemn this word because they apparently fail to discern some subtle distinction between the notion of human superiority over animals and the racist idea of white superiority over black. One wonders what Malcolm X would make of the comparison.) We treat animals differently because in this important respect we are not like them.

The one easy moral call in the great fur fracas is that uncontrolled trade in endangered species is indefensible, and almost everyone seems to agree on this. China recently turned down court appeals by two Sichuan farmers found guilty of selling four giant panda skins. With only one thousand pandas left in the wild, I have little spirit for opposing the death penalty, which is what the farmers got by way of a bullet to the back of the head. (Earlier they had gotten $17,000 in Canton for a single skin. My newswire source unfortunately doesn't indicate what the ultimate market price would have been or what depraved soul in the industrial world might have paid it.) Also, this year World Wildlife Fund investigators in Nepal documented a thriving trade in coats made from snow leopards and clouded leopards. They estimated that between seven hundred and one thousand threatened or endangered Himalayan cats were killed to supply the fur coats they saw.

In defending the American fur trade, it is important to keep in mind that for much of its history it was equally depraved. Hunters with specially trained dogs extirpated the sea mink from the North Atlantic coast in the 19th Century, leaving almost no record of how the species lived or what it looked like. The beaver and the sea otter barely escaped the same fate. Until conservationists mounted a successful protest in the late 1960s, the American fur industry also imported huge quantities of endangered spotted cats. But public opinion, strict new import laws, and the fur industry's alert attention to its own threatened survival changed all that, and the use of endangered species is no longer an issue in the American trade.

In truth, the legal skin trade is nowadays more likely to help save an endangered species than to wipe it out. The crucial difference is in how the trade is managed, and the American alligator is a case in point. Declared endangered by the U.S. Fish and Wildlife Service in 1967, it was a victim of reckless overhunting to supply the fashionable demand for alligator purses, belts, and shoes—products so frivolous as to lack even the socially redeeming potential of someday keeping homeless people in Grand Central Terminal warm.

Louisiana and Florida, the two states with a vocal alligator-hunting constituency, responded by investing heavily in recovery of the species. The result is that both states now have thriving alligator populations and a lucrative trade in skins. The trade is undoubtedly distasteful to animal rights activists, both on ethical grounds and, subliminally, because much of the money winds up in the pockets of crackers and Cajuns—the sort of people one does not find paying three dollars a glass for Perrier at a PETA rock concert. But here, as elsewhere in the world, giving locals a cash interest in protecting a habitat can benefit animals. When a landowner proposed a high-density waterfront development on Orange and Lochloosa lakes outside Gainesville, for example, the value of the alligator trade was one factor in killing the proposal and preserving the countryside. The trade has become a model program for the recovery and controlled exploitation of a species, and the alligator population is now healthy and growing rapidly.

Alligators are an admittedly imperfect model for the fur

trade. So let's talk instead about a warm, round-eyed furbearer in a leghold trap. Contrary to reputation, most trappers are not willfully cruel. If nothing else, they have a material interest in minimizing an animal's suffering. They do what they do to make a living, and they like to point out that they don't get paid for disembodied paws or damaged pelts. Such losses are the exception, and not, as animal rights activists suggest, the rule.

Where possible, trappers place their sets for mink, muskrat, and beaver underwater so the animal drowns within a minute or so of entering the trap. Increasingly, they use the Conibear trap, which is designed to kill the animal instantly. Under steady pressure from animal rights activists, manufacturers have developed better traps over the years—refining the trigger mechanism, for example, so that fewer nontarget animals get taken. Game departments have also promulgated stricter regulations, requiring trappers to participate in training or to check their traplines more frequently.

For many people this isn't enough. The sticking point is still what PETA calls "the merciless steel-jaw leghold trap," a primitive device which nowadays earns more money for animal rights groups than for trappers. PETA likes to distribute emotionally powerful photographs with graphic captions: "Animals caught in traps, such as this lynx, either die from exposure or starvation, chew off a limb and escape, or are bludgeoned to death by the returning trapper." Bludgeoning is, in truth, what happens, and while it may be quick, it is never pretty. Otherwise the leghold trap is less sensational than PETA might like. For want of a better alternative, even conservationists working with populations of endangered animals routinely use legholds, both the padded and the merciless steel-jaw, as the best way to trap an animal without hurting it. Researchers recently used padded legholds, for example, to trap lynx in Canada. They ran the trapline daily (as would a commercial trapper in this country), secure in the knowledge that animals of this size don't chew off their limbs, and are even less likely than a human to starve if left without food for ten or twelve hours. The lynx were transported to New York State and released unharmed to recolonize an old habitat.

This isn't to say that anybody (other than PETA fund-raisers) actually likes leghold traps. Used incorrectly, both padded and steel varieties can cause injuries and stress. But no one has yet developed a more effective alternative.

So why not just ban trapping outright and be done with it?

Apart from the lack of effect on our own way of life, such a ban is appealing mainly because of two emotional preconceptions, both erroneous: That furry critters are cuddly, and that the people who trap them are, in the words of a friend, "slack-jawed Neanderthals."

What the fur trade has here is a classic image problem, to put it in terms all Americans can readily grasp. The trappers I know are, by and large, intelligent, articulate people who love the outdoors. They are a lot like sport fishermen, who also lure animals with a bait and snare them, often ultimately bludgeoning them to death. The comparison is revealing: On the level of substance, as opposed to image, there is no material difference between fur trapping and sport fishing. And yet we regard fishing as an edifying pastime, a ritual for the bonding of father with son, or of man with nature. We celebrate it endlessly in our literature and in the catalogs of Orvis and L.L. Bean. The difference is purely a matter of unegalitarian mindset: For modern Americans, fishermen represent the educated elite out for healthy sport. Trappers represent the grubby underclass out for money.

The reason we should not end trapping is that we need these putative Neanderthals. In the muddled-up modern world, where all natural relationships have been banjaxed by human intervention, animal control is a fact of life. At a TSU demonstration in New York, a character with a megaphone led a jive-rhythm chant: "Holland's doin' it, why can't we? Make America fur-free!" It is perhaps a minor footnote (except to the Dutch), but Holland must still trap thousands of muskrats a year lest they undermine the dikes with their burrowing. Left to its own devices, nature would possibly work through such problems with normal boom-and-bust population dynamics. On the other hand, people tend to get impatient when forced to live for long periods on their rooftops.

In this country, farmers and highway departments, which are routinely flooded out by booming beaver populations, must routinely trap the animals even, as in the Mississippi Delta, where the fur is worthless. Wildlife refuges must trap coyote, fox, raccoon, and other predators, which can otherwise wipe out the concentrated nests of waterfowl and shorebirds. On the Louisiana coast, landowners (including National Audubon Society at its Paul J. Rainey Wildlife Sanctuary) must trap simply to keep the marshes from being nibbled bare of grass by muskrat or nutria and washed out to sea. Ending the fur trade wouldn't stop such

trapping. It would merely make it more costly. Instead of turning
the pelts into coats, we would probably send them up an incin-
erator smokestack, as we now do with the 7.5 million or so unwanted cats and dogs put down each year. A good solution for
protecting our own tender sensibilities, if not the environment.

We need these slack-jawed trappers because the rest of us have
become so suburban, so sophisticated, so caught up in the la-la
land of image and media, that we no longer have the first notion
of how the natural world works. Speaking for myself, I could not
tell the difference offhand between a gray fox and a red fox, or
whether one is booming and the other going bust. Frankly, I
empathize with the very likable TSU spokeswoman I interviewed,
who made the case that Louisiana's nutria problem would take
care of itself without trapping because, after all, the nutria had
always been there as a natural part of the environment. She was at
least a step ahead of most Americans, who don't even know that
nutria exist, much less that they were introduced to this country
from South America in the 1930s. She went on to suggest that
alligators would take care of the problem, if only hunters would
leave them alone. Why should she know, unless she were a trapper out in the field, that Louisiana alligators hibernate for six
months of the year and nutria don't? How would she know, unless
her work routinely took her into bayous swarming with rodents,
that not even alligators eat that much?

In reality the animals rights movement has elevated ignorance
about the natural world almost to the level of a philosophical
principle. In his book *Animal Liberation*, Peter Singer, the
movement's leading thinker, writes, "We tried to explain that
we were interested in the prevention of suffering and misery . . . Otherwise, we said, we were not especially 'interested in'
animals."

Indeed, many animal liberationists are quite frankly disdainful of such untrendy interests.

Trappers, by contrast, are hopelessly retrograde, caught up in
all the unfashionable minutiae of animal behavior, diet, habitat,
and seasonal change. Like many farmers, the better ones actually
love the animals they kill—and this obviously isn't the abstract
love, the passion for the helpless victim, of most animal rights
activists. In their obsessive attention to the nitty-gritty of animal
behavior and to the ups and downs of animal populations, they at
least have the potential to serve as antennae for the rest of us. In

British Columbia, for example, trappers, who work individual leases typically covering six hundred square miles, have become important adversaries of the clearcutting timber industry. They have negotiated with the loggers not to clearcut entire traplines. They have persuaded them to leave enough ground cover for voles and mice, so predators will come back into the area afterward. They have gotten them to replant aspen for beaver and to modify the spacing of seedlings so the wilderness doesn't become merely a tree farm. This role as environmentalist is one trappers elsewhere need to pursue far more aggressively in the war for public opinion.

As to the rest of us, I suggest that as long as the great fur fight continues, we follow the lead of a TSU marshal at the group's demonstration in New York. She showed up in what appeared to be a sealskin coat, with a "Fake Fur" sign pinned on the back to spare herself any unpleasantness. In the interest of facilitating snap moral judgments and helping people decide when to smile and when to glare, such signs might also read: "Fake Fur Made from Genuine Alaskan Oil," or "This Fur Trapped to Protect Sandhill Cranes at Malheur National Wildlife Refuge," or "Inherited This Fur from Grandma and Am Too Frugal to Junk It," or maybe even "Real Fur, but Homeless Person Within."

When everyone is properly labeled and we can figure out once and for all who is or isn't lowlife scum, maybe then we will be able to get back to the real business of saving the Earth from ourselves.

OUT OF THE CAGE: THE MOVEMENT IN TRANSITION[6]

The animal rights movement is winning! Incredible as it seems to some movement veterans, the idea of animal rights is already changing society as profoundly as the concepts of women's rights, ecology, and desegregation. Public sympathy is revealed in polls showing majority support for banning leghold trapping, ending cruel product testing, and having companion animals spayed and neutered; by bestselling pro-animal books such as John Robbins'

[6]Reprint of an article by Merritt Clifton. *The Animals' Agenda.* 10:26-30. Ja/F '90. Copyright 1990 by the Animal Rights Network, Inc.

Diet for a New America and Cleveland Amory's *The Cat Who Came For Christmas;* by the appearance of pro-animal themes on prime-time television; by the cautious identification of political figures with some of the movement's most popular positions.

Most of all, it's obvious the movement is winning from the scale and tactics of the counteroffensive launched against it:

• American Fur Industry president Elliot Lippin has vowed to "intimidate and harass" activists, as the fur trade spends triple the total budget of all anti-fur campaigns trying to defend itself.

• The pharmaceutical industry has formed a well-endowed coalition to "direct public relations and legislative activities" in support of the avowedly anti-animal rights aims of the National Association for Biomedical Research.

• The American Medical Association, boasting of having "led the battle against anti-vivisectionists years ago," has adopted an action plan calling for "development of legal means for contesting the tax-exempt status of animal rights groups"; "formation of a special investigative unit within government to examine animal rights activities"; "building a private data base on animal rights activities"; and "development of a Foundation for Animal Health to attract funding away from animal rights groups."

• Trying to discredit animal defenders, one protest target, U.S. Surgical, hired undercover agents to coax an unstable fringe activist into placing a bomb at the company parking lot.

"One is honored by one's friends; distinguished by one's enemies," observed longtime FBI director J. Edgar Hoover, who distinguished the late Martin Luther King by similar aggressive efforts to discredit the civil rights movement.

Used to frustrating uphill struggle, 50 national animal rights group leaders were somewhat surprised to be confronted by the movement's success at a recent planning workshop hosted by *The Animals' Agenda.* The message came from the outside perspective of Social Movement Empowerment Project analyst Bill Moyer, a lifelong student of how change happens, who had never before been involved with animal rights. Based upon nearly 30 years' close observation of the civil rights, antinuclear, and antiwar movements, Moyer unequivocally placed the mainstream of the animal rights movement close to the mainstream of western public consciousness.

"Remember," Moyer stressed, "movements for social change are by definition efforts based on widely-held fundamental values, such as being kind to animals and the preservation of life on the planet. Because these values are already fundamental to our society, you are not on the fringe. You are not outside the social milieu. Even though you are seeking specific major changes in how our society operates, you are part of the social mainstream and you will have public recognition and support in proportion to your ability to help the rest of the mainstream recognize the contradictions of their already-held values in their present lifestyle."

In Moyer's observation, social change movements progress through eight stages of activity. In the first stage, a relatively small number of people recognize that a problem exists. In stage two they attempt redress through existing channels and are rebuffed, because the "powerholders" hold the trust of a majority of the public. Stage three is a phase in which the opposition gradually gathers support, as more people respond to the problem and to the failure of the status quo to do something about it. Stage four comes as catalytic events bring the cause to public consciousness, and turn opinion in favor of the movement. New organizations spring up, mass marches and demonstrations are staged, and the status quo launches a counteroffensive.

At this point, Moyer sees movements either bogging down in a fifth stage of burnout and despair, when the stage four turning point fails to bring immediate change, or making a leap to stage six, where "the movement undergoes a transformation from a spontaneous protest movement to a long-term popular struggle to achieve positive social change."

During stage six, Moyer explains, "a new social and political consensus grows that erodes the powerholders' ability to continue their policies." Ironically, turnouts for mass marches decline, along with membership in militant front groups, but the movement gains strength at the grassroots, where primary objectives are implemented by countless established local and regional bodies—town councils, school boards, scout troops, and, in this case, humane societies. This leads to stage seven, the consolidation of objectives through the national political process, and stage eight, in which the movement ensures that newly won goals are not lost to backlash, and "circles back" to pick up further dimensions of the struggle that must now be advanced from earlier stages.

Pointing out that social change movements tend to include many submovements, each progressing at a different pace, Moyer sees components of the animal rights movement at every stage.

But the mainstream, he believes, is even now leaping from stage four to stage six; activists should neither be distracted nor discouraged by their passage through and around stage five.

Similar optimism comes from Michael O'Sullivan of the World Society for the Protection of Animals, who has had frequent contact with Third World animal rights movements now confronting the same situations our forebears did in the 19th century.

"I don't think we have to worry very much about the counteroffensive," O'Sullivan counsels. "In the first place we have the moral momentum. We know what they're trying to do to us, and why. In the second place, we are creative, energetic people, used to working under difficult circumstances with limited resources for long hours without seeing immediate results. There is nothing the animal exploitation industry can do to make life hard for us that we're not already used to dealing with. We wouldn't be here if we got discouraged in an unequal battle. Finally, we're right. Our opponents can't hold their positions with the tenacity we can, and can't get the good feeling we do by saying and doing what we do. In a psychological war of attrition, we win."

Part of the stage four to stage six transition involves restructuring organizations to empower the grassroots, integrating newcomers into the struggle, broadening movement influence, and bringing the movement closer to the public. Argues Keith Akers of the Vegetarian Union of North America, "I do not think it is possible to create a lasting movement for social change through elitism. It is possible to create such a movement by encouraging grassroots democracy, both within the movement and in society at large."

However, Akers notes, "Democracy takes practice. You can't just say, 'Now we're going to be democratic,' and do it. There is a need to approach this task carefully and sympathetically," which requires what may be termed a feminization of leadership.

This does not necessarily mean women replace men as the heads of organizations, though they may. It does mean that the charismatic, confrontational style of leadership effective in the earlier stages of the movement yields to a nurturing, coalition-building style that reunites what once was a dissident cause with a realigned social mainstream. As the social mainstream edges closer to accepting movement positions, the dramatic gestures once appropriate to awakening consciousness can become alienating and counterproductive.

During this feminization process, it is natural and understandable that some leaders who played the charismatic authority role during early movement stages may feel betrayed as "their" movements leave them behind. Such feelings can produce factionalism. As well as putting a more friendly face on the movement as seen by outsiders, nurturing democratic leaders must find means of gently persuading the old autocratic leaders that the time has come when compromises can be negotiated from strength, not weakness, that the purr can now be more effective than hissing with a rake of the claws, and that the transition of the movement does not mean the charismatic leaders are no longer loved and appreciated. They still have a job, but it's now less the job of hero than that of a wise parent who knows when to stand back and how to set a positive role model.

Changing Roles of Activism

Along with the feminization of leadership, the movement leap from stage four to stage six requires the maturation of individual activists in their relationships to society. Moyer has identified four roles of activism—played by groups as well as individuals—each with a positive and negative side, each with a vital function in achieving social change. Though activists are often limited to one role, ideally each person would be able to utilize them all, interchanging the roles to accommodate changing circumstances.

Most activists begin as normal "citizens" who become appalled at specific moral failings of society. Awakened to these systemic ills, one may adopt the role of "rebel," "social change agent," or "reformed"; but for some activists, playing the role of "citizen" can be a primary function that provides "legitimacy" to movement positions in the public eye. The role of citizen has a perilous downside, however. These movement conservatives can be so attached to social values and so threatened by nonconformity that they get in the way of movement progress. Yet, citizen is a role Moyer discourages activists from abandoning altogether. "Activists need to be perceived as solid citizens if they are to be acceptable to the general population."

"Rebels," who are typically but not exclusively the idealistic young, pose an open, obvious direct challenge to the way things are. Often the challenge spills over from one injustice, for instance a classroom dissection lab, to many aspects of the society condoning that injustice. As Rosa Feldman of the Student Action Corps for Animals points out, "Students who refuse dissection are breaking new ground in changing human attitudes about whether animal lives can merely be used and thrown away. . . . Students who refuse dissection are refusing the act of animal exploitation *and* refusing the learned mindset that allows school sponsored animal exploitation to be considered normal and necessary. Many students find themselves in the painful self-questioning process of where to draw the line in their stand, or even if there is a line to be drawn." Beginning with refusal to dissect, the young rebel may rapidly progress to other animal causes; and upon meeting opposition from school and parents, may identify rebellion against animal abuse with more general and typical adolescent rebellion against all authority.

The rebel role can be catalytic, especially since it is in this phase that the newly awakened individual is most likely to perceive the connections between specific abuses and general habits of society. The rebel is most sensitive to hypocrisy, the failure of society to fulfill professed values and ideals. However, the rebel role becomes counterproductive if at any point the individual, or group, begins to run on negative energy, becoming anti-everything instead of pro-positive alternatives. The rebel must learn to say not only, "This is wrong," but also, "This is what we can do about it, and here's how."

As "social change agents," the maturing rebels first propose and then demonstrate alternative models. As "reformers," onetime rebels learn to operate within the system, to make change happen through the very political process they once rejected. The risks for social change agents are utopianism or failure through excessive ambition and inexperience; for reformers, the risks are co-option by the status quo, a willingness to compromise too much, or the acceptance of inadequate reforms that actually block further advances by the movement.

Opposition Tactics

Feminization of leadership and maturation of activism should allow the movement to sidestep its aggressive opponents, whose strategies depend upon scaring the public with images of activists as negative rebels. "To defeat the animal rights movement," states the AMA [American Medical Association] Animal Research Action Plan of June, 1989, "one has to . . . isolate the hardcore activists from the general public and shrink the size of the sympathizers. . . . The animal activist movement must be shown to be not only anti-science but also responsible for violent and illegal acts . . . and a threat to the public's freedom of choice (to eat meat, wear furs, attend rodeo, etcetera.)" The May, 1985 document *Defense Of The Fur Trade,* prepared on the advice of Thomas Grey Inc. by the Canadian Department of External Affairs, outlines a similar strategy of attempting to dilute, divert, divide, and dissipate the animal rights movement by trying to link its mainstream concepts with the more extreme acts and positions of the most militant fringe. Linking animal rights to violence can be accomplished only through legally-actionable slander and innuendo, and the deeds of *agents provocateurs* such as those who set up the U.S. Surgical bombing attempt. This movement grows out of a long explicitly anti-violent tradition embraced by such figures as Thoreau and Gandhi. No one has ever been killed in the name of animal rights, though animal rights proponents have been killed defending animals; and the AMA's list of 50 break-ins that took 2,000 animals from labs over the past ten years approximately equals the annual activity of cattle rustlers in any major ranching state. The movement has overwhelmingly taken to heart and followed the 106-year-old creed of the American Anti Vivisection Society, "You cannot do Evil that Good may result," while rejection of that creed is the very cornerstone of the opposition's contention that possible benefits to people warrant cruelty.

Otherwise, the opposition is attacking in areas where general support for animal protection is strong and the ultimate success of movement aims seems inevitable: the use of animals in science, for food and clothing, and for entertainment.

Attempting to portray the animal rights movement as anti-science runs afoul of mounting scientific evidence, including from the most prolific and aggressive vivisectors, that animals feel physical and psychological pain. It is inherently self-contradictory for the biomedical research industry to claim both that animals are appropriate models for testing cures for humans, and that the subject animals do not suffer as we do. Within the movement are a legion of credentialed scientists and physicians, supported by others completely outside the movement, who advance non-animal research models as both better science and more efficient use of tax dollars. Even the Chemical Manufacturers' Association contends in a current lawsuit that animal testing is not an accurate or appropriate means of assessing human health risks. It is possible that as Bina Robinson of CIVIS [anti-vivisection group] contends, "The tide against animal experimentation has already turned."

Attempting to cut animal rights activists off from mainstream society by pointing out that they're against eating meat overlooks the fact that vegetarianism and even veganism have quietly entered mainstream lifestyles, for a combination of economic, health, and ethical reasons. A single vegetarian cookbook, *Laurel's Kitchen*, has sold more copies than the combined membership of every animal rights group. Beef and pork consumption per capita has declined in the U.S. every year of the 1980s. A confrontation over meat-eating may be just what activists want.

Notes Akers, "In my opinion there is essentially one major animal issue, the suffering and death of animals for food. There are few kinds of animal exploitation that cannot be convincingly defended, provided that one makes the concession that it is all right to eat meat."

"We see the problems of farm animals as a top priority," agrees Henry Spira of the Animal Rights International Coalitions, "because 95 percent of all animal suffering in the U.S. is in factory farming. More than five billion farm animals suffer from birth to slaughter each year. Thus, every one percent reduction in their suffering can accomplish more than all other animal campaigns put together."

A confrontation over meat-eating could become the last stand of animal-exploiting industries, for as Susan Smith of the Farm Animal Reform Movement writes, "Hardly a week passes without a news report on the effects of fats, cholesterol, carcinogens, antibiotics, hormones, and even genetic manipulation of farm animals on consumer health. Other stories recount the rising cost of food, water pollution, depletion of topsoil and groundwater, loss of wildlife habitat (to farming), spread of world hunger (largely due to the diversion of grain crops to feed livestock), and incidents of farm animal abuse. Each such event presents a unique opportunity to advance our view. Ultimately our view will prevail, if only because we will run out of the resources required to sustain animal agriculture or because the American people will get tired of getting sick and dying prematurely."

Even if the hamburger and chicken merchants are still wringing out record profits, the argument that activists are anti-meat is by now unlikely to cause most of the aware, voting public to do much more than shrug and maybe ask for recipes. For that reason, at least six animal rights groups now publish recipe books, cards, or newsletters.

Finally, the cruelty to animals who are confined in zoos or

flung to the ground in rodeos is obvious even to the smallest child who asks why that big kitty is kept in a cage or why the man is beating up the calf. In asking the public to boycott such abuses, animal advocates are not attacking anyone's freedom to choose; they're asking their fellow conscientious citizens to exercise choice in ending atrocities many have condoned only because they haven't previously noticed them.

Specific Movement Strategies

While feminization of leadership and maturation of activism are trends underway across much of the animal rights movement, individual groups look to the 1990s with a variety of unique initiatives. Of particular long-term significance may be those of the Association of Veterinarians for Animal Rights, Farm Sanctuary, and WSPA—who are, respectively, two of the smaller groups in the field and one of the largest.

Charging that the American Veterinary Medical Association puts ethical concern for animals below making money, at cost to public trust in vets, AVAR is in the midst of a three-year plan whose objective is "promoting responsibility toward the non-human patient as the way to enhance" the veterinary image. Implicit in this campaign is the belief that at least a majority of humans who take animals to vets have already accepted that animals have rights, even if the AVMA has not. In this sphere, anyway, animal rights has already advanced from transition to influence.

Farm Sanctuary's shelters for abused livestock actively encourage visitors, who see firsthand the individuality and intelligence of animals when they aren't treated as mere abstract units of production. Located out in the country, the Farm Sanctuary shelters also pose a moral challenge to farming neighbors, many of whom share revulsion at how animals are treated in modern commercial agriculture. "We don't pretend we can rescue all farm animals," says co-founder Lori Bauston, "but the mere fact we're doing this," one of the most unabashedly idealistic projects in an idealistic movement, "makes a lot of people take notice and think."

Extending humane education and anti-cruelty campaigns into Africa and Latin America, WSPA seeds the notion of animal rights among societies whose economic infrastructure is yet to be developed. Though the trends in Third World development have

thus far been discouraging, mostly emulating our own rape of the
wilderness and the Industrial Revolution, such Western-style development hasn't yet raised most Africans and Latin Americans
out of poverty. It is still possible, and urgent, given the global
importance of southern hemisphere rainforests, that future development will take a more gentle direction. In societies still dominated by tribal worldviews, but also still inclined toward animism,
animal rights could help bring about ecological consciousness essential not only to the survival of endangered animals, but to the
survival of both Third World peoples and, ultimately, ourselves.

BIBLIOGRAPHY

An asterisk (*) preceding a reference indicates that the material or part of it has been reprinted in this book.

BOOKS AND PAMPHLETS

Baird, Robert M. & Rosenbaum, Stuart E. Animal experimentation: the moral issue. Prometheus Books. '91.

Birch, Charles & Cobb, John. The illustration of life. Cambridge Univ. Press. '81.

Boyd, B. R. The new abolitionists: animal rights and human liberation. Taterhill SF. '87.

Clark, Stephen R. The moral status of animals. Oxford Univ. Press. '84.

Collard, Andree, and Contrucci, Joyce. Rape of the wild: man's violence against animals and the earth. Indiana Univ. Press. '89.

Cook, Lori. A shopper's guide to cruelty-free products. Bantam. '90.

Covino, Joseph, Jr. Lab animals abuse: vivisection exposed! New Human Press. '90.

Dickenson, Lynda. Victims of vanity. Sterling. '89.

Dolan, Edward F., Jr. Animal rights. Watts. '86.

Dunstan, G. R., and Maurice, F. D. Science and sensibility. State Mutual Bk. '82.

Fox, Michael W. Returning to Eden: animal rights and human responsibility. Krieger. '86.

Fox, Michael W. Inhuman society: the American way of exploiting animals. St. Martin's Press. '90.

Garattini, S., ed. The importance of animal experimentation for safety and biomedical research. Kluwer Academic. '90.

Godlovitch, Roslind & Stanley, & Harris, John. Animals, men and morals: an enquiry into the mal-treatment of non-humans. Taplinger. '72.

Harrison, Ruth. Animal machines. Stuart. '64.

Hearne, Vicki. Adam's task: calling animals by name. Knopf. '86.

Howard-Moineau, Henrietta. Teaching humane education: animal welfare issues. Hampshire Press. '83.

Hyland, J. R. The slaughter of terrified beasts: a biblical basis for the humane treatment of animals. Viatoris Ministries. '88.

Kass, Leon. Toward a more natural science. Free Press. '85.

Leahey, Michael P. T. Against liberation: putting animals in perspective. Routledge. '91.

Linzey, Andrew. Christianity and the rights of animals. Crossroad NY. '87.

Livingston, John A., et al. Skinned: activists condemn the horrors of the fur trade. International Wildlife. '89.

Loeper, John J. Crusade for kindess: Henry Bergh and the ASPCA. Atheneum. '91.

McKenna, Virginia, et al., eds. Beyond the bars: the zoo dilemma. Harper & Row. '88.

Magel, Charles R. Keyguide to information sources on animal rights. McFarland & Co. '89.

Midgely, Mary. Beast and man: the roots of human nature. Cornell Univ. Press. '78.

Miller, Harlan B., and Williams, William H., eds. Ethics and animals. Humana. '83.

Office of Technology Assessment. Alternatives to animal use in research testing. Dekker. '88.

Paterson, David, and Palmer, Mary, eds. The status of animals: ethics, education and welfare. CAB Intl. '89.

Phillips, M. T., and Sechzer, J. A. Animal research and ethical conflict. Springer-Verlag. '89.

Regan, Tom. The case for animal rights. Univ. of California Press. '83.

Regan, Tom, ed. Animal sacrifices: religious perspectives on the use of animals in science. Temple Univ. Press. '86.

Regan, Tom, and Singer, Peter. Animal rights and human obligations. Prentice-Hall. '89.

Rodd, Rosemary. Biology, ethics, and animals. Oxford Univ. Press. '90.

Rohr, Janelle. Animal rights: opposing viewpoints. Greenhaven Press. '89.

Rollin, Bernard E. The unheeded cry: animal consciousness, animal pain, and science. Oxford Univ. Press. '90.

Rothschild, Miriam. Animals and man: the Romane lecture for 1984–5. Oxford Univ. Press. '87.

Rowan, Andrew N. Animals and people sharing the world. Univ. Press of New England. '88.

Rowan, Andrew N. Of mice, models, and men: a critical evaluation of animal research. State Univ. of New York Press. '84.

Ryder, Richard A. Animal revolution: changing attitudes towards speciesism. Basil Blackwell. '89.

Sapontzis, Steven. Morals, reason, and animals. Temple Univ. Press. '87.

Serpell, James. In the company of animals. Basil, Blackwell. '86.

Singer, Peter. Animal liberation. Avon. '77.

Singer, Peter. In defense of animals. Harper & Row. '86.

Steffens, Bradley. Animal rights: distinguishing between fact and opinion. Greenhaven. '89.

Wynne-Tyson, Jon., ed. The extended circle: a commonplace book of animal rights. Paragon House. '88.

ADDITIONAL PERIODICAL ARTICLES WITH ABSTRACTS

For those who wish to read more widely on the subject of animal rights, this section contains abstracts of additional articles that bear on the topic. Readers who require a comprehensive list of materials are advised to consult the *Reader's Guide to Periodical Literature* and other Wilson indexes.

RIGHTS AND RESPONSIBILITIES

Dolphin defense. Dwight Holing. *Discover* 9:68-72+ O '88

The U.S. Navy's Marine Mammal Program, which operates out of secret facilities in California, Florida, and Hawaii, has been studying the possible military uses of dolphins and other marine mammals since 1960. The military is interested in dolphins because of their streamlined shape, high speed, and uniquely sensitive sonar capabilities. Military-trained dolphins were initially used to carry messages, mark mines, and retrieve equipment. During the late 1960s, however, the Navy began training dolphins to detect mines and intercept enemy divers. Trained dolphins were reportedly used during the Vietnam War, and today a team of five dolphins helps patrol the Persian Gulf. Although the Navy contends that the marine mammals in the program are treated well, the idea of military dolphins has alarmed some civilian scientists and animal rights activists.

Hunter sabotage. Douglas Starr. *Omni* 7:20+ O '84

Inspired by animal protection groups in England and Canada, the American animal rights movement has turned militant. Members of groups such as Friends of Animals and the Coalition Against Sport Hunting have attempted to attract attention to their cause by harassing hunters, frightening off game, and damaging hunter equipment. More radical offshoots such as the Animal Liberation Front defaced fur store windows and sabotaged animal laboratory experiments. The Wildlife Legislative Fund, a hunting lobby, and similar groups have expressed outrage at the acts. Conservation groups such as the National Wildlife Federation, which perceive hunting as sometimes beneficial to animal populations, also object. Legislation prohibiting harassment of hunters has been passed in ten states and similar bills are pending in ten others.

But animals rights activists remain undeterred and promise continued civil disobedience.

Ethics and animals. Steven Zak. *The Atlantic* 263:68-74 Mr '89

The Constitution should extend the same protection to animals as it does to humans in order to halt the exploitation of animals in research labs. Current mores and laws hold that torturing animals to no purpose is wrong, but torturing them for the purpose of making scientific discoveries is equally indefensible.

The view that scientists should not be constrained in their search for knowledge is fallacious. In fact, science has always worked under economic, social, and ethical constraints, some of which have actually freed scientists to seek knowledge in areas that might have remained unexplored. If animals were protected by law from scientific exploitation, researchers would have an incentive to find alternatives to animal research. Until such a law is enacted, the animal-rights movement will by definition remain radical and can be expected to engage in illegal activities.

Animal rights and wrongs. John R. Cole. *The Humanist* 50:12–14+ Jl/Ag '90

Animal rights are a more complex issue than absolutists on both sides of the debate will admit. Animal rights activists are wrong to claim that no harm or perhaps even inconvenience is ever justified, but some animal research advocates likewise oversimplify if they argue that virtually all experiments are conscionable and that civilians should stay out of the way.

Do animals have rights?. Ingrid Groller. *Parents* 65:33 My '90

A national public opinion poll commissioned by Parents magazine reveals that most Americans believe in animal rights. Sixty-three percent of the respondents said that killing animals to make fur coats should be prohibited by law, and fifty-eight percent said that using animals for cosmetic research should be illegal. The majority of those polled accepted the killing of animals for food and the use of animals in medical research.

Behind the laboratory door. Peter Haskill Bresnick. *The Progressive* 54:20 Mr '90

Part of a cover story on animal rights. Only one federal law directly defines the rights of laboratory animals, and animal rights activists maintain that it is ineffective. According to a researcher for People for the Ethical Treatment of Animals, the law makes no restrictions on the experiments themselves. To remedy this situation, animal rights activists are working to reveal to the public what goes on behind laboratory doors.

Animals and ethics: a Catholic blind spot. James Gaffney. *America* 163:297–9 O 27 '90

Catholic moral theology can no longer ignore the field of animal ethics and the duties of human animals toward nonhuman ones. According to at least one study, Catholics fall behind other Christian denominations on a scale of moral interest in the treatment of animals, and they are more apathetic on the issue than either Jews or members of Eastern religions. Catholics will most likely begin to show an interest in the field now that the status of animals is debated as a serious ethical dilemma in other segments of society. One place to start a Catholic reflection on the issue is with St. Thomas Aquinas and St. Thomas More, who hold that cruelty is a moral vice and one that can be perpetrated on animals. Inflicting pain on animals, therefore, is not an indifferent matter, and it requires a moral justification that cannot always be found.

An uncaged vision of nonhuman creation. James M. Wall. *The Christian Century* 106:947–8 O 25 '89

Anglican theologian Andrew Linzey challenges conventional attitudes toward animals and argues for the extension of rights to all living creatures. Basing his work partly on the thought of Karl Barth, Linzey asserts that humans and animals alike share in God's love. He condemns the use of animals in scientific research on the assumption that their lives have only utilitarian value. Medical scientists and others who lobby for research programs worry that the efforts of Linzey and his colleagues in the animal rights movement will undermine or halt research. Linzey counters that inadequate efforts are being made to find alternatives to animal experimentation.

ANIMALS IN RESEARCH

Inhuman bondage. Mike Sager. *Rolling Stone* 86–8+ Mr 24 '88

The Animal Liberation Front (ALF) is an underground terrorist organization that advocates an end to all human exploitation of animals for any purpose. The group was formed in England in 1972 as the Band of Mercy and assumed its present name in 1976. The American arm was founded in 1982. Since then the American ALF has played on the public's growing concern about the treatment of animals in laboratories, using the spectacle of crimes like raids on research facilities to both free animals and win attention and converts for their cause. The work of Australian author Peter Singer has also increased the ranks of animal rights advocates. An ALF raid on a U.S. government research facility in Maryland is also described.

Test tube toxicology: new tests may reduce the need for animals in product safety testing. Rick Weiss. *Science News* 133:42–5 Ja 16 '88

New in vitro tests promise to provide alternatives to using animals in product safety testing. Participants at a symposium at the Johns Hopkins Center for Alternatives to Animal Testing (CAAT) noted that more than 100 in vitro toxicology tests are under development. The CAAT focuses entirely on the study of new methods for testing the safety of household chemicals, cosmetics, and therapeutic products. The cosmetic industry is also working on in vitro alternatives. Companies are learning that in vitro tests are cheaper and can yield more precise results than animal tests. The CAAT symposium provided an update on the status of in vitro skin and life toxicity testing and featured Living Skin Equivalents, which are growing masses of living human skin. Some researchers and animal activists complain that federal regulatory agencies are failing to provide the necessary guidelines that could eventually lead to standardization and widespread use of in vitro tests.

Blood feud. Deborah Erikson. *Scientific American* 262:17–18 Je '90

Animal researchers, who have long been the target of animal rights activists, are beginning to fight back. Universities are tightening their security measures and devising crisis management plans, scientists are taking courses on dealing with the media and the Foundation for Biomedical Research has prepared a series of television advertisements on the benefits of animal research. The Alcohol, Drug Abuse and Mental Health Administration is funding fellowships for selected scientists who will travel the country explaining the need for animal experimentation. Three bills that would protect animal research facilities are under consideration in the Congress. Nevertheless, some fear that these efforts may not be enough to offset the well-organized animal rights movement.

Jane's dilemma. Sy Montgomery. *Buzzworm* 3:34–5 My/Je '91

Jane Goodall continues to work with chimpanzees for their survival and better treatment. Goodall began studying wild chimpanzees in the Gombe Stream Reserve in Tanzania 30 years ago. In 1986 she published a monumental scientific work, The Chimpanzees of Gombe, which summarized her findings. She also founded the Committee for the Conservation and Care of Chimpanzees with the goal of providing scientific data to support strict international protection for wild chimpanzees and improvement in the physical and psychological care of captive chimps. Goodall now spends most of her time lobbying senators, giving press conferences, making television appearances, delivering lectures and visiting zoos and medical laboratories. Her intimate individual relationship with chimpanzees informed her science and is now animating her crusade.

Why animal experimentation should continue. Karl Biermann. *The Humanist* 50:8–9+ Jl/Ag '90

Part of a cover story on animal rights. Animal research is in the best interests of animals as well as humans because scientific advances have benefitted both groups. People should ask themselves whether the welfare of laboratory animals is more important than the welfare of all the people and animals whom research can benefit.

Taking the offensive for animal research. Julie Ann Miller and Carolyn Strange. *BioScience* 40:431 Je '90

Participants of a session of use of animals in biomedical research at the New Orleans meeting for the American Association for the Advancement of Science agreed that researchers must take an offensive stance against the increasing interference from the animal rights movement. They emphasized the need for the biology community and perhaps the entire academic community to speak out against what some scientists consider to be a fundamental attack on academic freedom. Researchers should become active rather than reactive and should support responsible research using animals. They must avoid the trap of using medical relevance as a defense and support colleagues who are targeted by animal rights activists. Moreover, the public should be educated about biomedical research. One proposal under consideration would establish fellowships so that scientists can engage in public education and leadership activities.

THE MOVEMENT IN TRANSITION

In defense of the animals. Meg Greenfield. *Newsweek* 113:78 Ap 17 '89

Animal rights activists, who advocate the liberation of laboratory animals and often champion the claims of animals over humans, have earned a reputation as fanatics. As in other movements, however, zealots are necessary to alter the sensibility of the masses, and much of what the animal activists say is right. Some human interests should not take precedence over animal concerns. For example, much painful and crippling experimentation on animals has taken place not just for medical research but for the creation of luxuries and superfluous vanity items. Although zealots may reject the middle ground—the belief that animals can be used for some purposes without being made to suffer horribly or gratuitously—they can be credited with bringing many people to this reasonable position.

The killing game. Joy Williams. *Esquire* 114:112–16+ O '90

Sport hunting is immoral and should be made illegal. Each year, hunters kill some 200 million birds and animals on millions of acres of land in the United States. Much of this land, including national parks, state forest preserves for hunters and national wildlife refuges, is maintained with general taxpayer revenues. Hunters who account to only 7 percent of the population argue that they are conservationists, and some downplay the killing part of hunting. Nevertheless, the main attraction of hunting is the pursuit and murder of animals. Americans should stigmatize hunting and should cease to regard it as recreation or sport.

Animal rights vs. hunters. Walter Howard. *Outdoor Life* 187:110–11 Ap '91

Animal rights advocates don't have an accurate understanding of the reality and cruelty of nature. Thinking that they are acting on behalf of the welfare of animals, animal rightists religiously oppose hunting as a barbaric intrusion. They don't see that predation by humans is the only way to maintain healthy population levels in any native animal species. Animal rightists believe that pain, as long as it is not inflicted by man, is natural. Man is a part of nature however, and as such is responsible for assisting in the control of animal populations in environments that man has modified. Luckily man can assist nature through hunting, a process that causes less suffering for animals that self limitation and pays for more research into their conservation.

Uncle Sam's war on wildlife. Michael Satchell. *U.S. News & World Report* 100:36–7 F 5 '90

Part of a cover story on the ethical aspects of hunting. The U.S. Department of Agriculture's Animal Damage Control (ADC) program has drawn criticism from many animal rights activists. In 1990, the program will spend $29.4 million in federal funds and about $15 million in state funds to kill mammals and birds considered predators or pests. Critics view ADC as a misuse of public funds and fear that it threatens the mountain lion and black bear populations in several western states. Proponents argue that the problem protects farmers and holds down food prices.

Saving creatures great and small. *U.S. News & World Report* 105:13 D 5 '88

Animal rights proponents have scored a spate of victories against researchers who use animals in their laboratories. After an 18-month protest by a small group called Trans-Species Unlimited, a professor at Cornell University Medical College abandoned a 14 year project involving feline barbiturate addiction and returned $600.00 in grants to the National Institute on Drug Abuse. His decision marked the first time that an experiment was halted directly as a result of pressure from animal rights groups. The University of Cincinnati has also halted a 14-year feline study that involved crushing cats' skulls to simulate human skull trauma. Benetton Cosmetics has agreed to stop using animals in product testing, and this week the U.S. Fish and Wildlife Service will recommend that wild chimpanzees be placed on the endangered species list, a move that will encourage efforts to place captive chimps in the same category.

Pressuring Perdue. Barnaby Feder. *The New York Times Magazine* 32+ N 26 '89

Henry Spira, one of the original motivators of the growing animal rights movement, is now turning his attention to the treatment of animals in barnyards. He has charged Frank Perdue of Perdue Farms of grossly misrepresenting the conditions under which the company's chickens are raised and slaughtered. He is forming a campaign with other animal rights activists to boycott Perdue and publicize the treatment of chickens and other farm animals. In the past, Spira has successfully lobbied to reduce the number of animals maimed and killed in medical research and product testing. A vegetarian, he would like society to stop eating meat and killing animals for fur.

An uneasy dip with the dolphins. Eugene Linden. *Time* 134:80–1 N 27 '89

Some conservationists are critical of commercial swim-with-the-dolphin programs. The critics see the programs as an instance of people depriving highly intelligent animals of their freedom and putting them at risk of disease or mishandling. The National Marine Fisheries Service is currently studying the issue to determine whether it should revise the way it permits private interests to use dolphins.

Animal testing for cosmetics safety is under fire, and critics are demanding new and better alternatives. Rachel Urquhart. *Vogue* 180:230+ N '90

Using animals to test the safety of cosmetics has long been controversial, and it has come under increasing fire in the last ten years. Only 1 percent of the animals used in laboratories are used to test cosmetics, but many animal protectionists say that animal testing of this sort can be replaced by alternative tests that don't involve animals. Animal-testing advocates, however, argue that sentimentality should not get in the way of testing, which they see as crucial to ensuring consumer safety and continuing progress in product development. While no one denies that the testing causes animals pain and death, the two sides don't agree on how soon the alternative tests can be phased in and to what degree animal testing can be reduced. The mere fact that alternatives to animal testing are discussed represents progress, however, and a general interest in both human safety and responsibility to animals seems to be defusing the politics that used to fuel the issue.

Lifting the curtain on animal labs. Belton P. Mouras. *USA Today* (Periodical) 116:48–51 Mr '88

No longer the anti-science faddists of years past, today's animal rights activists are science-oriented crusaders against experiments that unnecessarily inflict suffering on animals. The activists acknowledge the benefits offered by modern medical science but deplore the widespread tendency toward duplicative, gratuitously violent animal experiments and object to the secrecy that often surrounds them. Computer simulations, mathematical models, and other alternatives to animal experimentation have been used to good effect and deserve to be investigated further. The proposed Life Sciences Center at the University of California at Berkeley would be an ideal setting for such study.

Animals in research: the case for experimentation. Frederick A. King. *Psychology Today* 18:56–8 S '84

Animal research has been an integral factor in many scientific advances and should not be prohibited in order to protect animals at the expense of further breakthroughs. The Mobilization for Animals Coalition (MFA), an animal-protectionist network, has made groundless charges of inhumane treatment of animals in scientific experiments, particularly those in psychological research. The MFA seeks to bar the type of research that has enabled scientists to understand, for example, how to use biofeedback to control blood pressure and pain. Most scientists responsibly follow the federal guidelines that set standards for the care of research animals. Humane treatment of animals is important, but human welfare must be the overriding issue.

Reducing the need for animal testing. Richard C. Thompson. *FDA Consumer* 22:15–17 F '88

As the agency that regulates a broad range of products, the FDA is concerned about the growing controversy over the use of animals to test the safety and effectiveness of new products and procedures. The FDA's position is that, until more effective alternatives are found, animal testing of new products is necessary to minimize health risks to humans. FDA regulations concerning animal testing rely on the Animal Welfare Act of 1966, a law designed to prevent the unregulated capture and sale of certain animals for research purposes. The act has been amended several times to extend protection to various species. In a 1986 report, the Office of Technology Assessment discussed alternatives to animal use such as substituting experimental methods that do not require animals, reducing the number of test subjects, and refining the methods to minimize animals' pain and discomfort.

THE MOVEMENT IN TRANSITION

Animal abuse: a difficult problem. Richard H. Pitcairn. *Prevention* 39:65–7 Je '87

Animals are often subject to battering and abuse. Madeline Bernstein, vice president of humane law enforcement for the American Society for the Prevention of Cruelty to Animals in New York City, and Michael W. Fox, scientific director of the Humane Society of the United States, consider pet abuse to be a major problem in U.S. households. Well-intentioned owners may mistreat pets by abandoning small animals they have brought into vacation houses, confining an animal in a hot car, failing to recognize symptoms of illness, or leaving a highly social animal alone for long periods. Others may abuse pets by redirecting their anger at another person toward a helpless animal or by carrying out occult practices involving the sacrifice and torture of animals. Bernstein recommends that people who see or suspect animal abuse lodge a complaint with their local enforcement authority rather than attempt to intervene directly.

Keeping 'em down, on the farm. Carollyn James. *Science 84* 5:77–8 S '84

As farming has evolved into a big business, many farmers have instituted animal husbandry techniques designed to squeeze the highest profits out of their stock. Cattle, dairy cows, poultry, pigs, and other farm animals are confined and quickly fattened in rigidly monitored pens. The U.S. Humane Society and other animal activists maintain that farm animals deserve the same legal protection from abuse that pets and research animals have. The activists aren't trying to deny farmers the right to earn a living by raising animals, but they are concerned about animal management practices that have turned farms into food factories where the welfare of animals is not given consideration. Until legislation is passed that will force farmers to use more humane methods of animal husbandry, activists are asking the U.S. consumer to be a vegetarian or conscientious omnivore in the hope that farmers will get the message.

Guess what's coming to dinner? Factory farming and your food. Bill Gupton. *Utne Reader* 43-6 S/O '88

Excerpted from the January 16, 1988, issue of Atlanta's Creative Loafing. On today's poultry farms, chickens are raised in super barns that are rife with disease. More than 100,000 chickens may be housed in a single building. Overcrowding, stress, and lack of exercise cause disease, so farmers routinely feed their flocks antibiotics and other drugs that can be harmful to humans. The widespread use of antibiotics is also dangerous because it leads to the development of drug-resistant strains of bacteria in animals. USDA inspectors at meat-processing plants are expected to determine which birds are diseased, but they spend an average of less than two seconds examining each chicken. In any case, they can't detect the drugs that the birds have been fed, which is potentially the most dangerous threat. Some agricultural scientists now advocate experiments in irradiation to combat the problems that have been caused largely by modern farming practices.